Hungry for love

Hungry for love

Debbie Lovell

Inter-Varsity Press

INTER-VARSITY PRESS
38 De Montfort Street, Leicester LE1 7GP, England

Bible quotations marked NIV are from the Holy Bible, New
International Version. Copyright © 1973, 1978, 1984
International Bible Society. Published in Great Britain by
Hodder and Stoughton Ltd. Those marked GNB are from the
Good News Bible (Today's English Version) published by The
Bible Societies and Collins © American Bible Society, New
York, 1966, 1971, 1976.

British Library Cataloguing in Publication Data
A catalogue record for this book is available from the British
Library.

ISBN 0–85110–875–X

Set in Linotron Bembo

Typeset in Great Britain by Parker Typesetting Service,
Leicester

Printed in Great Britain by Cox & Wyman Ltd, Reading

Author's royalties from the sale of this book are donated to the
Universities and Colleges Christian Fellowship and Anorexia
and Bulimia Care.

*Inter-Varsity Press is the book-publishing division of the Universities
and Colleges Christian Fellowship (formerly the Inter-Varsity
Fellowship), a student movement linking Christian Unions in
universities and colleges throughout the United Kingdom and the
Republic of Ireland, and a member movement of the International
Fellowship of Evangelical Students. For information about local and
national activities write to UCCF, 38 De Montfort Street, Leicester
LE1 7GP.*

Contents

Part One: A personal story

Part Two: Offering and finding help

Part One

A personal story

Hungry for love

Strive for perfection (2 Corinthians 13:11, GNB).

I was born a perfectionist, arriving exactly on the pre-
dicted date! I have heard it said that I did not speak until
I had mastered the rules of grammar, and although my
parents had thought that I might be behind normal
development as I was so quiet, there was no catching up
to be done when, as a two-year-old, I suddenly started
producing immaculate sentences. I continued to aim for
perfection at school, striving to achieve gold stars and
good report cards. Even competing in the 'monkey
race' on sports day was taken very seriously by me – the
parents were amused by my look of grim determination
as I scrambled along on all fours, crossing the finishing
line long before the other children. This was the only
race in which I excelled, and so I had no great desire to
compete in the other events. To come last would have
been humiliating. I even felt a failure when I failed an
eye-test and had to begin wearing glasses.

I did not have many intimate relationships as a child.
In fact, my parents have told me that I used to claim my
best friend was a gnome which lived at the bottom of
the garden, and that I spoke more to this gnome than to
any person. My other close friend was a lollipop-man,
who helped children to cross the busy road on which we
lived. My mother always made him a cup of tea during
the afternoon, after he had taken the youngest pupils
across the road and was waiting for the seniors who
came out of school slightly later. I liked carrying his
drink out to him and having a chat. I did also have one
special friend of my own age who attended the same

playgroup as myself. We were very pleased to find that we were in the same class when we started school at the age of five, but our friendship came to an abrupt end the next year, when we were six, when her family moved house and she left the school. By that time relationships had already been established among the other class members, and I was reluctant to make a special effort to become close to anyone because I had discovered that friends can disappear. I started to work very hard, being anxious to gain the approval of my teachers rather than of my classmates.

Occasionally I did try to become accepted by my peer group by misbehaving in class, but I was too scared of getting into trouble to be very rebellious. On the whole, though, I was a bit of a 'teacher's pet'. It was probably for this reason, and also because I never 'told tales' or retaliated in any way, that I was bullied. I was in a composite class, with half of the class being one year older than I was and studying a different syllabus. It was a group of the older, bigger girls who mocked me. My mother told me that 'sticks and stones can break your bones but names will never hurt you', and so I tried not to listen to their teasing. It was, however, more difficult to ignore their actions, and I could not simply walk away when a scarf or a skipping rope was flung around my neck and I was told to 'giddy-up' or risk being strangled. The tight cord around my throat certainly made me feel a little hoarse, if not a little horse. But the main feeling which remained with me was one of inferiority, as I concluded that to be treated as an underdog must be all that I deserved. I believed that I must have a very unattractive personality because people seemed to hate me, rather than like me. My only consolation was that I was not fat, like the other girl in my year who was teased, and when sports teams were chosen, I would be picked before she was. Although I

10

felt a misfit when my unfashionable clothes were laughed at, my shape at least did not raise comments.

As I never took any measures to prevent the bullying, and instead came to expect it, it continued to take place, year after year. Nor was home a refuge from the fear in which I lived. I had developed a tremendous awe for my father. I do not recall ever being physically punished by my dad, and yet I was very scared of him. I always tried to be as quiet as possible when he was at home, to avoid the dreaded yell, 'Stop plonking!' I did my best to keep my bedroom tidy, knowing from my father's angry remarks about our generally cluttered living room that he strongly objected to untidiness. My mother had grown used to his criticism, but I feared it. When dad did scold me I felt broken inside, and so I tried hard to be obedient and to do well at school, in order to be praised. I felt that I needed to be good and successful in order to be loved, not understanding that my parents disciplined me *because* they loved me. I would speak to dad about important decisions, such as choosing which subjects to take at school, but I often felt that I needed a reason, and almost an appointment, to consult him.

My father was a Labour Party councillor, and had (so it seemed to me) innumerable council meetings to attend, as well as a surgery. I considered him to be a very busy and important man. My respect for him grew each time I heard him give an opinion on the radio, or saw him in the newspaper, or even on television. I was proud to have such a father, who was a man of real integrity; for example, my mother once picked some rhubarb from the garden of an empty house where it was going to waste, and my father referred to it as 'stolen fruit' and boycotted it. When I was feeling inferior I sometimes reminded myself that my father had stood for Parliament around the time of my birth, and that I myself had been pushed in my pram in Cardiff by James Callaghan, who was to become Prime Minister six years later. I also felt important when, at around six years of age, I played an active part in the local council election, squeaking 'Vote Lovell, vote Labour' through a megaphone.

I spent much more time with my mother than with my father, but did not show her any of the same respect. She was the one who gave me a slap when I deserved it, and yet I did not fear her as I feared my father. I tended to answer her back, and also to go to her with my questions and worries. My elder sister and I occasionally had a secret meeting in the airing cupboard where we said spiteful things about our mother, and we made up a language in which we could communicate without mum understanding, in an attempt to irritate her. In time I became very sorry for treating my mother in this manner. I made myself tell her 'I love you', as a way of apologizing, and also because I longed to hear the words which were spoken on American television programmes, 'I love you, too.' But our family is not a very expressive one (cuddles or hugs being very rare, and kisses being considered by mum to be unhygienic), and I had to make do with the curt response, 'Of course you do.' I could tell from my parents' actions that they loved their three children very much, but I was greedy for a more visible expression to confirm that love, as I felt unlovable.

My sister Heather was four year older than I, a sufficient age difference for us not to spend too much time together (the sessions in the airing cupboard being an exception), either quarrelling or playing. Heather started going to school when I was one, and soon had her own friends and interests. Around that time my mother would sing me to sleep with the words:

I have two little girls,
They are such precious pearls;
One is Cleopatra,
Who never gets any fatter.
The other is Helen of Troy,
Who should have been a boy.

There is a theory that anorexia nervosa is partly a result of fear of becoming a mature female. By starving herself, a girl can prevent menstruation and the development of feminine curves, and retain a more asexual, pre-pubescent body. It is possible that the trivial song, which I never forgot, had far-reaching consequences for me, making me afraid of becoming an adult woman. After all, through the song, Heather ('Cleopatra') had been praised for remaining slim, while I ('Helen') had been informed that I 'should have been a boy', the son my father had been hoping for. Although both parents did treat Heather and me as 'precious pearls', showing their care and not rejecting us in any way for being girls, the implications carried within the ditty may have had a lasting effect on us. I certainly was not looking forward to the time when I would become a mature woman. My father joked that he regretted having daughters because weddings are expensive for the parents of the bride – and so I decided never to get married. My mum was more serious when she expressed regret about the fact that her children were growing up. She still dreamt that she had a baby daughter when Heather and I were actually in our teens. She recounted the dreams in a wistful, nostalgic manner, which did not make accepting adulthood any easier for us.

When I was four, my brother was born. I was very disappointed when I was not allowed to see him during his first few days of life because he needed to be placed in an incubator in a special nursery as there had been birth complications due to a womb infection. When I was lifted up to look through the windows into the special nursery, I could see only a frightening amount of complicated equipment. It certainly did not resemble any of the nurseries which I had had fun playing in, and I could see no sign of a child. 'Fraser' was still only a name.

He soon came home, however, and I treated him as 'my baby'. It was wonderful to be able to 'help' mum to bathe and dress the new arrival, and within a few months I was allowed to take him out on my own, pushing him around the neighbourhood in his pram while I sang the little songs which I had learned at playgroup. I continued to look after him as he grew up. I even volunteered to play in goal when Fraser started to play football, taking it upon myself to be my 'brother's keeper'. Naturally, however, the time came when he got embarrassed about having his big sister around, and he informed me that he was big enough to look after himself. He reinforced this by calling me 'fat and ugly, with glasses', leaving me to weep privately in my bedroom, feeling that even my family could not accept me. I blamed myself when Fraser started to threaten to 'run away from home', and even packed a little suitcase and stomped out of the door with it, although he went only to the end of the road before returning. I realized that I would have to let him grow up. I forgot about his insults until after my experience with anorexia, when my mother, looking for causes in an attempt to understand the confusion which had enveloped my life, suggested that Fraser's words might have been a contributory factor. All the causes for the development of a problem such as anorexia cannot be pinpointed, but the feeling that I was worthless, which an accumulation of events in early life left me with, prepared the way for my future self-denial.

Another factor was my perfectionism. When I took part in inter-church Bible quizzes, I memorized whole chapters of the Bible to ensure that I would be able to answer any question posed. I also put a lot of effort into entering competitions, and I built up a collection of prizes won for stories, poems and plays which I had written. In the musical sphere, I sang in the annual regional music festival, coming second every time and feeling somewhat disappointed instead of being pleased; my sister nearly always won her section. I usually did better at talent contests in the holiday camps we stayed at during the summer. One memorable summer we stayed in two different camps, and entered a talent contest in each. My sister was the winner and I took second prize in the first camp, and our positions were reversed the following week. I did feel some sympathy for the other contestants, but even holidays had become times to demonstrate achievement.

I eventually felt that I was getting too old to perform like a musical box, singing for an audience. In the last talent contest which I entered, each contestant was given a sweet for participating, and there were no other prizes. I felt that I had not sung well, and was very upset about this although it meant nothing at all to anyone else. Being so achievement-orientated, I became very annoyed with myself whenever I did something badly. I decided that I did not deserve the sticky toffee, and because everyone in the family refused to take my prize from me I threw it away. I disliked waste, but would not accept a prize which I felt I should not have received. Being given something for taking part, for being yourself, was a concept which I did not understand. As I saw life, you were rewarded only when you were a success.

At school I began to condemn myself whenever I failed to get top marks. I believed that my parents loved me more when I did well. Hadn't they stopped my ballet classes when I was eight because I was only getting a 'pass plus' result in my exams? When I achieved 98% in a mock O-grade examination, and my mother asked 'What happened to the other 2%?', I saw her comment not as a joke, but as a way of saying that I was not good enough. I became angry with myself for not doing better.

I longed to make myself lovable, and wanted to be noticed, which, as a quiet girl, I often was not. Even my achievements did not seem to gain me much attention, as good marks were merely expected in our family. As a pre-schooler I had once pretended that I had been sick, and had attempted to colour some water with my felt pens to convince my mother that it was vomit, in order to gain some sympathy and be in the spotlight. In my teens I was much more sophisticated in my approach, but still yearned for people to acknowledge my presence as I stood on the bathroom scales, sighing 'When I get down to seven stones, perhaps they'll notice me.'

2

Why was I born?

I despise myself (Job 42:6, NIV).

Listening to my grandparents I discovered that my mother and my father had been surprisingly similar in their early years. My parents were serious children. Both had learned to read when very young, and had spent time studying alone rather than playing with other children. While his brothers played outside with friends, my father used to create mathematical problems with playing cards or used matches, or to sit talking about political issues with the knowledgeable gentleman who lived next door. He had a constant desire to learn, and he read virtually every book in the school, which meant that the headmistress had to bring in extra books for him. He was the first pupil from the school ever to pass the eleven plus examination and proceed to grammar school – where he met my mother. Although they came from large families and money was tight, both of my parents managed to go on to university. My father became a university lecturer. My mother taught languages for several years, but gave up teaching before starting a family and became primarily a homemaker.

Like my parents, I treated life as a serious matter. Nevertheless, I did also have a tremendous sense of fun in my early years, and can remember the delight of fooling my family with my 'April Fool' tricks. Summer holidays in particular were very special times. Travelling on the sleeper-train to Hampshire each year I would be too excited to sleep much, and would lie in wonder watching the country rush past. I tended to enjoy the 'adult' part of the holiday, visiting relatives, far more than my brother and sister, who found all the talking rather boring and much preferred the picnics, fun-fairs, and games of crazy golf. My grandparents, aunts and uncles were wonderful people to spend time with, as they were fun-loving, caring and generous. I was pleased when they commented on how grown up I was.

I certainly had a more mature attitude to life than that expected of a child of my years. While my peers chanted, 'Twinkle, twinkle little star, How I wonder what you are . . .', I learned to recite instead,

> Scintillate, scintillate glow-ball vivific,
> Fain would I ponder thy mystery specific,
> Loftily poised in the ether capacious,
> Strongly resembling a gem carbonaceous.
> Scintillate, scintillate glow-ball vivific,
> Fain would I ponder thy mystery specific.

My precosity, if that is what it was, did not stop at a delight in long words. Thirsting for knowledge, when I was given a children's encyclopaedia I began to read it from cover to cover, although I eventually put it aside without finishing it and read other books instead. (One of the books which captured my attention was called *How You Began*, which my parents had also given me for my seventh birthday so that they could teach me the facts of life without having to talk about the embarrassing subject.)

I enjoyed keeping secrets, knowing something that others did not know, such as a surprise planned for someone's birthday. I bought gifts long before I intended to give them, and hid them away. Unfortunately, however, I was not merely secretive, but was also deceitful. One day, after an argument, I wrote 'Deborah is a pig' on my sister's bedroom door in the hope that she would be blamed. (Heather had recently

18

written a description of me for her homework, which she ended with the words, 'and when she cries she looks like a pig' – words I could not forget.) My family had already encountered my deceiving ways when at the age of three I stole a sweet from a corner shop. I do not think that I actually realized I was doing wrong, until my mother, suspicious, inspected my bedroom. I guessed that she was looking for the sweet and hid it in my doll's house. When mum finally gave up the hunt I showed her the hidden sweet, feeling very guilty. For a punishment I was made to eat the thing which by now I hated, and I almost choked on the large gob-stopper. I sucked it with a lump in my throat, feeling thoroughly ashamed, as my mother stood over me watching. She then took me back to the shop, and made me slip money into the cash-box as secretly as I had previously slipped the sweet out of the shop. In this way the theft was paid for without my mother having to admit to the shop assistant that one of her children had stolen, which would have been a disgrace for the family.

If I did not have a developed sense of conscience at the start of that episode, I certainly did by the time it was over. Nevertheless, that was not the last occasion on which I stole. When I was about seven, I took money from mum's purse. There was a craze for football stickers at school, and I had noticed the attention which children with good collections received. With the stolen money, I was able to accumulate dozens of these stickers. I had little interest in them for themselves, but I thrived on the attention which they brought me.

But the attention did not last long, and was in any case no compensation for the feelings I was left with after stealing. I developed an intense self-hatred which remained with me for many years. I considered myself to be worthless, useless and bad, and wished that I had never been born. I sometimes slapped or scratched

19

myself in anger, and occasionally felt an impulse to jump out in front of a car, but knew that this would be wrong. I wondered if there was any way in which I could accidentally kill myself, perhaps by living dangerously. I would experiment to see how long I could hold my breath for, but I never even felt faint after trying. I was ready to die, and already had written down that I wanted to donate to others all my body organs which could be of use, while the remains could be handed over for scientific research so that no funeral would be necessary.

My self-hatred became apparent to others during one task which I was given at school. I was told to take the letters of my name, Deborah, and find a word which described me beginning with each letter. I started with the last letter, 'H', and without hesitation wrote 'H is for horrible'. My teacher thought that perhaps I had been unable to think of any other adjectives beginning with that letter, but I assured her that I had chosen the word 'horrible' because I believed that this described me, not because I could not think of alternatives.

I summed up my feelings in the words, 'I'm a reject – send me back to my manufacturer.' Although I was always terrified by the thought of rape, death held no fear for me, seeming instead a wonderful escape from a world of suffering and sorrow.

3

I don't deserve food

'No,' said Peter, 'you shall never wash my feet'
(John 13:8, NIV).

I went through childhood believing that I did not deserve treats. I was quite content to wear clothes selected by my mother at jumble sales, or passed down from my sister, and I sometimes got upset if I was bought anything which I did not need, feeling that the money was being wasted on me. Our family tended to give useful gifts rather than frivolities in any case, and I was not surprised when I received items such as washing powder, tea-towels, a toothbrush or shampoo for Christmas. When I received something which I classed as a luxury, there was a strong chance that I would put it in a drawer and later give it to someone else – not because I did not like it, but because I felt I had no right to it. Even the 'birthday sweet' which I was given at primary school and the bar of toffee which I won in a monkey race were given away, and I used to enjoy keeping my Easter eggs until my brother and sister had finished theirs and then sharing mine, in return for favours from them.

Self-denial was a way of life for me. I very rarely spent pocket money on anything for my own pleasure, instead splitting it equally between money for the church offering, for gifts and stamps, for holiday money (to be spent on presents for others), and savings to be put in the bank (from where they never returned as I never withdrew cash from my account).

I could sing with meaning one of my favourite songs, 'Close every door to me, hide all the world from me', from the musical *Joseph and the Amazing Technicolor Dreamcoat*. My other favourites were equally melancholy – 'Where is love?' from *Oliver* (which I much preferred to the more famous song in that musical, 'Food, glorious food'), 'Maybe far away' from *Annie*, and the lyric 'Nobody's child'. All of these are sung by lonely orphans.

Once, for a school assignment, I was required to write a letter to *Jim'll Fix It* expressing the dreams which I wanted to come true. I was incapable of performing this task, as I could not think of any treat which I would be worthy to receive. My teacher was startled by my inability even to begin this simple exercise, as I was usually a willing and able pupil. I was myself puzzled by the fact that everyone else in the class had wishes which they wanted to be granted but I did not.

My deep-felt belief that I did not deserve anything good was perhaps expressed most poignantly in my private prayer that someone else would be given my 'ticket to heaven' if this was possible. Although Jesus promised eternal life to those who believe in him, and I did trust in him, I felt I had no right to go to heaven if other people were going to hell.

Although I tried to bring happiness to other people, and often made funny remarks (my superficial joviality being partly an attempt to hide my insecurity), because of my somewhat ascetic principles I must at times have been a misery to live with, putting a damper on celebrations. For instance, when out for a meal with my family I always chose the cheapest dish on the menu. I often went for the prawn cocktail, a starter, instead of a main course. I also ate anything left over by the rest of the family, and any rolls which came free with the meal. My mum was quite pleased at my cheap choices, always selecting an inexpensive main meal herself, but my father thought that I was a bit of a 'meany', a miser.

Although we could choose our menu when dining out, eating at home was a different matter. My mother brought Heather and me up with the rule 'Eat it whether you like it or not.' Perhaps this was a result of a 'famine mentality' which she acquired through experiencing rationing during the Second World War. Certainly it differed from the 'throwaway' values most of my friends were taught by their parents, who were born after the war.

Fraser escaped from the 'Eat it' regime as he was a sickly baby and mum was glad to see him eat at all, fearing that he might not survive for long. He became a fussy eater who refused to touch most vegetables, secretly passing them to someone else if our father insisted that he be given a few greens. He often asked for baked beans on toast in place of the meal which had been prepared for the family. Heather and I, in contrast, ate whatever was put in front of us.

As cooking was not really mum's forte, we tended to live on food from tins and packets. A home-made meal consisted of steak from a tin covered with a packet of pastry rolled out at home! I came to consider food wastage a major crime, and ate everything provided at school dinners as well as at home. Fraser did not share my scruples about wastage, and was delighted when at a Christmas party (and wearing my best clothes), I sat down on a plate of sausage rolls which he had placed delicately on my seat while I had been standing pouring out drinks!

During my secondary school years I began to think about people who had to survive with much less to eat than I had. Heather went off to Birmingham University when I was fourteen, and, seeing my mum send her tea-bags and packets of Cup-a-soup, I concluded that students must exist on very little money and hardly any food. I decided that it would be a good idea for me to practise reducing my intake as a way of preparing for life as a student, and possibly life as a missionary overseas in future years. (As a pre-schooler I had attempted to prepare myself for the future, after learning about war rations, by storing sugar lumps under my pillow as a way of 'saving up for the shortages'.) In preparation for future scarcity I stopped taking second helpings at school meals (although, unlike most pupils, I actually enjoyed school lunches), and I cut out snacks.

Around this time the famine in Ethiopia began to hit the headlines, and I was very upset when I saw pictures of people starving while I had so much. I was disgusted by the waste and extravagance evident all around me while people were starving overseas. Many adolescents develop extreme humanitarian or political ideas, as they become aware of injustice in the world and want to do something to change it. I was no exception. I could not ignore the plight of the poor. I asked my parents not to give me any Christmas presents, donating the money to famine relief instead. They would not comply with this request, gently pointing out that they were already giving money to help the starving, and they liked giving gifts to their children, treating the three of us equally, and seeing us enjoy receiving them. When the appeals for aid for the hungry were at their height I participated in a sponsored fast to raise funds. Some people whom I asked to sponsor me, including my father, voiced their disapproval (for health reasons) at the concept of a fast. Nevertheless, I was not forbidden to go ahead, and so I went through twenty-four hours consuming only water. I was glad to have this opportunity to raise money, and felt that I had learned in a very small way what it is like to be hungry, remembering the scorn with which my sister had once said to me, when I complained about a meal being late, 'You have never been hungry.' Aware that fasting is a biblical principle,

I was sure that I was right to participate, and I volunteered for similar events in the future. Going without food can leave one feeling 'high' (because of the endorphins produced by the body), and I started to experience the reinforcing effects of short-term food deprivation which I became accustomed to later as an anorexic.

Every year during Lent mum was in the habit of giving up some item, such as chocolate or cheese, in memory of the sacrifices which Christ made for us, and of his forty days spent in the wilderness. Any money saved in this ways was given to a charity. Considering this a great idea, at the age of twelve I had given up sweets for Lent. I did not eat much confectionery anyway, and felt proud to be able to do without it. When Easter arrived to mark the end of Lent, I had no desire to start eating sweets again, enjoying demonstrating the strength of my will-power by continuing to abstain. I accepted the chocolate Easter eggs which I was given, but gave my brother the contents from the centre. I did not eat sweets again until after my time in hospital with anorexia, more than four years later.

The following Lent I wanted to think of something else to give up, and so I decided to abstain from all items containing chocolate. I also went without a school lunch one day each week, although I had previously eaten a school meal every school day since the age of six. My sister had suggested the idea of missing school lunches during Lent, and our mother donated the money which was saved in this manner to a good cause. I took a bag of crisps to school on these days for my lunch, and ate very slowly, sucking the flavour out of each crisp to make them last. As had been the case the year before, I did not resume my usual habits after Easter. I continued to resist chocolate, although I did re-commence having school lunches every day. I felt that I was being very healthy in refusing sweets and chocolates, and my dentist congratulated me on the condition of my teeth. I received books instead of Easter eggs for Easter.

It became progressively harder to choose something to give up for Lent on succeeding years. Crisps went one year, and biscuits and cakes the next, although I did eat cakes again after Easter, to the relief of my mother who was running out of ideas of what to feed me on Saturday and Sunday evenings, when we generally had sandwiches, crisps and cakes.

After learning in biology and food and nutrition lessons about the effects of fatty foods, I became anxious to reduce the amount of fat in my diet. My father spoke about high cholesterol levels and the advantages of healthy eating, which motivated me further in my efforts to cut out fat. My opinion of school dinners rapidly fell, as, it seemed to me, they *always* managed to produce chips or some other unhealthy item. I still felt obliged to eat the whole meal because my mother was paying for it. My diary for this period is unbelievably boring to read, but does illustrate my concerns at the time. My social life, if it existed, hardly receives a mention. Saturdays tend to be recorded as 'orchestra and homework', and Sundays as 'church and writing letters'. On a typical school day I wrote down a list of the lessons, followed by a comment of the sort 'Horrid greasy chips for lunch again.' I had begun to look for a way to avoid the types of foods with which I was uncomfortable.

4

Fading

I groan aloud; I am nothing but skin and bones
(Psalm 102:5, GNB).

A woman's only power is the power of refusal
(Jane Austen).

Many of my teenage school companions spoke about
going on diets, but I cannot remember one point when I
consciously decided to reduce my weight. I had never
been fat (although my brother had called me fat in order
to insult me). In fact, my mother had been concerned
that I was failing to thrive when at around the age of
eight I weighed only three stones, although I had been a
big (eight pounds) baby. The school nurse had assured
mum that there was nothing to worry about.

I was not very concerned with my appearance. I never
knew what the current fashion was. With straight
brown hair, brown eyes, freckles and hairy legs, I
considered myself ugly; but I never bothered to try to
alter my appearance, for example by changing my
hairstyle. The only exception was one night during my
early years when I attempted to cut my own hair
because I was hot, managing to remove one large square
from my fringe! I thought that I looked slightly better
without my National Health Service spectacles, but
decided that buying contact lenses instead would be an
unjustifiable extravagance. I did not use make-up either,
for the same reason. In fact, I was under the impression
that there was something 'wrong' or 'false' about
cosmetics, as I knew that my father disapproved of
them. As a five-year-old I had refused to wear make-up

when I performed in a dancing show, declaring that I was probably 'allergic' to it. I was not quite sure what this meant, but it had the desired effect. Anyway, I was playing a tea-bag, and who has ever heard of a tea-bag wearing make-up?

I was aware that my mother was on the large side and that she frequently tried to follow different reducing diets. I wanted to make sure that I did not become fat and so become, like mum, the butt of my father's jokes. The funny little poems which I wrote in home-made birthday cards often included a reference to fatness or thinness, suggesting that this was often on my mind.

When I was sixteen, I suddenly realized how I could get away without eating the whole meal at school dinners while not wasting the money which my mother paid for them. The answer was simple really – I offered to control the lunch queue and collect the tickets, gaining in return a free lunch. It was great to be able to choose what I wanted for the meal, which meant no chips and often no pudding. As long as my mother had been paying for the meal I had felt under obligation to eat everything provided, but now I was free from her restrictions. People who have had to obey others tend to rebel when given the opportunity, and this is what I did. I did not tell my mum that I was no longer eating the whole meal. I did not directly lie about my behaviour either, and convinced myself that I was doing nothing wrong. When mum asked the question which she had repeated almost daily since I started school, 'What did you have for lunch today?', I would reply, 'There was . . .', followed by a list of what was on offer, deliberately neglecting to add that I had not taken everything! I saw this not as deceit, but simply as a means of avoiding an argument. I felt unable to eat the whole meal any more, and I reasoned that no-one was hurt this way. I felt guilty when I ate, considering

28

myself greedy to have even the items which I accepted; and guilty when my family got upset because I was not eating well. The only solution seemed to be to pretend that I was eating more than I actually was.

I managed to persuade my mother to let me prepare my own meal on the evening each week on which I returned home after the rest of the family had eaten, having been at an orchestra rehearsal. I was allowed to have just a poached egg on toast, as my mum believed that I had eaten a big lunch at school and I insisted that I did not need two big meals every day. My 'big' school meal sometimes consisted of several helpings of vegetables. In my distorted view I was eating a lot, but when my brother ate his packed lunch in the dining room (mum never having managed to persuade him to tackle the school meal) his report to mum of how much – or rather how little – I had eaten was not consistent with my own view.

The Scottish O-grade examinations were the major hurdle of this year for me. Although I was involved in several church activities, I spent a lot of time working for my exams. I was rewarded by a grade one, the top grade, for each of my eight subjects. I 'swotted' even harder in the year which followed, in preparation for my higher exams. I still had little confidence in my academic ability, never attributing any success to my intelligence, although I was sure that when I did not do well it was because I was stupid. I believed that I could succeed only if I worked exceptionally hard, memorizing as much as possible to make up for my limited understanding.

By the time my higher exams were only three months away, many people were expressing concern about how thin and pale I was looking. I felt that they were making an unnecessary fuss. I could see that I was thin and so I concluded that I could not be 'anorexic', a word which had started to crop up. But I did not consider myself to be outstandingly underweight. Nevertheless, I allowed my mother to take me to see the doctor, because I was sure that nothing was wrong with me and I wanted mum's mind to be put at ease. I knew that she had begun to worry about my weight and had started to read books about anorexia, although my parents, like myself, had for months denied that there was a problem. I told the doctor that I had not had a period for six months, and asked if this might be because I was underweight. The doctor took my weight and height, which were 6 st 4 lbs and 5 ft 4 ins, and confirmed that the amenorrhoea (as it is called) was indeed probably due to my low weight. As anxiety can also affect menstruation, I was given a twofold prescription: eat a bar of chocolate each day, and go out and relax at parties more!

This prescription would have delighted many teenagers, but I hated the sound of it. Chocolate had not passed my lips since Lent three years earlier, and when a person with will-power as strong as mine decides to give something up, it can be a hard job to persuade her to accept it again. Mum bought my 'medicine' for me on the way home from the doctor's – a bar of 'Fruit and Nut' which I chose in the vain hope that it would contain more fruit than chocolate. I shut myself in my bedroom and cried before I managed to swallow my pride and two chunks of the chocolate. Feeling sick, I went to report that I had done my best and had eaten enough of it for that day. I would not have thought, at this stage or later, of throwing the food away or making myself sick. The chocolate went into the fridge, and a bar a day became a bar a week, with my brother sometimes helping me to finish it. Mum seemed to be pleased just to see me trying, and encouraged me to keep up the effort. The one reason that I was glad about seeking medical advice was that the doctor had commented, 'At least you're definitely not anorexic – you are far too cheerful for that.' My façade of happiness had concealed the fact that underneath I was screaming for help. Although I refused to think about the possibility of having anorexia, I had sub-consciously dreaded that that was what the diagnosis would be. When the doctor dispelled this possibility I felt extremely relieved and light, almost walking on air.

Extremely light I was, but over the next few months I became lighter and lighter. Every so often someone would look at my skinny figure and exclaim in disgust, 'You're anorexic, you are!' I already had anorexic thoughts, and because other people accepted that I was anorexic and expected me to behave accordingly, I started to act on my impulses instead of fighting against them. At home, for example, I began to mix hot water with my milk before drinking it or pouring it on my cereal. I called this 'wilk' or 'morter'. Gradually the amount of water increased and the volume of milk decreased, until I was drinking hot water. (I already tended to avoid tea and coffee, considering them to be drugs.)

We rarely ate together as a family. I can even remember my mother instructing me, 'Eating, like going to the toilet, is something which should be done in private.' Usually my brother ate in one room while watching the television, mum ate separately while reading the newspaper, while I was left to eat in the kitchen (like Cinderella, my father would say), studying my books. Dad tended to return from work after the rest of us had finished our meal. Any time I could give some of my portion to him I would do so, even if it meant waiting until mum had dished out my meal and left the room, and then opening the oven door and returning some of my portion to dad's dish. I rationalized that this

31

was the right way to act as I did not deserve the food and dad did.

I was, as one doctor said later, a 'smart cookie', and I was able to deceive myself as well as deceiving those around me. In order not to lie, I sometimes ate a crumb of bread or cheese so that I could say that I had eaten a 'piece' of it, without mentioning what size this 'piece' was. I got some satisfaction from such 'games'. By this stage I had persuaded mum to allow me to take a packed lunch to school on the days on which I could not get a free school meal. This worked well for me until the day mum looked inside my sandwiches to find a trace of margarine and the tiny sprinkling of cheese which I had included so that I could honestly say that I had made 'cheese sandwiches' if she asked. Mum threatened to prepare my lunch for me in future, and I felt horrified as I pictured the huge hunks of cheese which she customarily consumed. Much to my relief, the threat was not carried out. I already tended to offer other people parts of my lunch, such as packets of peanuts which mum often included. I simply felt unable to eat as much as she wanted me to, and believed that it would be wrong and greedy to do so. No amount of pressure can make an anorexic overcome such thought patterns; there are many barriers in the way which need to be removed before she can see her situation as others see it.

I compromised on the doctor's advice to eat more, and also on the second part of the prescription, that of going to parties. I reckoned that I had too much studying to do to think about parties. I tried to keep Sundays free from work, but with that exception I was a dedicated 'workaholic', even studying on Christmas Day. I read textbooks not only at the meal table, but also in the doctor's waiting room and in the bathroom. I always left something to read in the bathroom, hiding it under the bathmat so that the room did not look untidy. A group of about six friends whom I often sat with in lessons, most of them, like myself, members of the school Christian Union, invited me to join them on Friday evenings when they spent time together, meeting in each of their homes in turn. Although I might have enjoyed an occasional evening off studying, I resented it when my mother insisted that I had to join my friends. I went out as commanded . . . but so did my books. One evening I revised maths while the other girls watched a video, although I could hardly see the writing in the dark! I also occasionally studied in the dark in my bedroom, after my mother thought that I had gone to bed. I was determined to do well in my exams, and felt secure when I was working hard, believing that this was the way in which to gain praise and acceptance. Unwilling to let mum rule my life and yet believing disobedience to be wrong, I obeyed her in letter, going out to parties as she instructed, but when I got there I did not relax and join in the fun and laughter as she intended me to. As my mother had even taken a book to her wedding reception, and read on her honeymoon, I did not feel that she had a right to tell me to leave my work at home.

I had not really been overprotected as a child. Nevertheless, as a teenager I may subconsciously have thought that mum was 'smothering' me. On two occasions I woke in the middle of a dream in which she was holding a blanket over my face, not allowing me to move or to breathe. The second time I woke with the thought, 'Mum is suffocating me!' This idea shocked me, and I hated myself for permitting it to surface and tried to forget it. I was not willing to concede that my parents could have faults as well as merits. When a doctor who attended my church tried to help me acknowledge my feelings, by pointing out a failing in my mother and stating, 'That would make me angry if she was my mother', I recoiled from even the thought of anger, conceiving it as an unacceptable emotion unless the object it was directed at was myself. Similarly, I felt it would be wrong to dislike anyone at all, and I convinced myself that it was my fault if I found it difficult to get on with anyone.

I would not rebel directly against my parents as some teenagers do, and so I rebelled against food instead. By rejecting the food my mother and father provided for me, I fought in a subtle way against their influence on my life. In my struggle to gain control over my own life, it is not surprising that food became the battle area. Food had been the cause of bitterness and conflict between my mother and myself on a few memorable occasions in my childhood. This included the time when I had drawn a picture with my dirty finger in my brother's baby-milk and had been punished by being forced to eat the whole tin of milk powder with my soup. The 'Eat it whether you like it or not' rule had also caused friction when it was first enforced. Now I decided that my food intake was one thing which I could control myself, although I might have to deceive my mother to prevent her from intervening. And so I played tricks, such as putting a biscuit wrapper on the table so that mum would know I had eaten a biscuit (although I didn't actually *say* I had done so) . . . and later retrieving the wrapper from the dustbin and leaving it on the table again.

A yearning for control, feelings of unworthiness, a desire to prepare myself for future 'shortages', a wish to be noticed and a determination not to become fat, were probably all reasons, conscious or subconscious, for limiting my food intake at various times. I could also give more than one explanation for increasing the amount of exercise which I took. The reason which I gave to myself and others at the time was that I arrived at places more quickly by jogging than by walking, and so wasted neither time nor the money necessary for buses. I jogged the mile and a half home from school, with a heavy bag of books over my shoulder, so that I arrived home in time to study before my meal. Although I was offered a lift to school most mornings, I started to prefer walking instead, to 'clear my head' and 'get more fresh air'. At weekends I would take a short jog and then do sit-ups and press-ups in my bedroom, so that I could say 'Yes' when my father, himself a marathon runner, enquired, 'I hope you have not been working all day – have you taken any exercise?' I knew that dad admired runners, and that he had been pleased when I was the first to finish a cross-country run at school. I wanted to be fit and tough, and full of stamina. The only thing which I disliked about running was being seen. Often children jeered and shouted insults as I plodded past them. Looking back, I think it is likely that it was my scarecrow-like frame which caused attention, but at the time I put the comments down to my overall ugliness, and I despised my body, and wished that it would disappear. I wondered what it would be like to be really invisible. As I felt very unsure of myself and anxious to please, I paid attention to every remark made about me.

I felt like I was juggling several eggs at once as I tried to please my parents, and keep up my Christian activities, and make decisions about my future, and prepare for the exams which were approaching all too quickly. In fact, everything seemed to be moving too rapidly, as if I were trapped in the middle of a tangle of fuses burning to their ends, fizzling towards me from all directions. On top of everything else, people were obviously concerned about my weight loss, and my mother was especially unhappy.

I was very confused about what was happening to my

35

life, and was unwilling to allow my thoughts to focus on my situation. Jogging along, with a hypnotic rhythm, it was easy to keep at bay the thoughts which tended to intrude when I spent time walking. Sometimes as I jogged, words from a poem which I was studying at school came into my mind: 'I will not think, I will not think until I have to.' Exercise helped anaesthetize my mind from painful thoughts. By jogging home I also escaped from the company of my school companions. One of my closest friends had recently left the area. Another friend with whom I used to walk to school had stopped speaking to me through some misunderstanding – I did not know her reason for suddenly ignoring me, and as this had never happened to me before I felt bewildered and perplexed. At the same time I was relieved that I no longer had to engage in conversation on the way home, as I felt uneasy with people, and was losing the ability to communicate, withdrawing further and further into myself.

Although I used every means I knew of to prevent myself from thinking about what was happening to me, as my weight continued to drop my body forced me to take notice. Having lost the warmth provided by body fat, I felt cold, and I huddled up against my radiator to study in the evenings, allowing my baggy pullover to cover my frail frame. A nurse described me as 'paler than pale'. Smiling became painful, as there was little skin free to stretch and I could feel my skin tighten against my cheekbones. My lowest vertebra appeared to poke right through my skin, causing bleeding when I jolted up and down doing sit-ups. My knees were weak, and sometimes gave way while I was running. Some of my body's reactions to undernutrition frightened me and increased my disgust with myself. I started to lose my balance and occasionally fell over in the street; although grazed, I would rise feeling not pain but shame. I experienced a temporary dizziness (known as 'orthostatic hypotension') when I moved quickly from a sitting to a standing position. Sometimes I woke up and found that I was completely unable to move, although I knew that I was awake because I could hear everything around me and after a few moments I would be able to jolt myself into action. This lack of co-ordination scared me, although I tried not to listen to the voice in my head which suggested that it might be a result of my failing to eat enough for my brain to function properly.

My voice had become a monotonous, depressed drone, and I was no longer able to sing in tune. Hair had begun to fall out in handfuls. I became constipated, and started to add bran to my food in an attempt to remedy this, although I never resorted to taking laxatives. But what horrified me most was the discovery that I was losing control over my bladder. I found myself rushing home and reaching the bathroom only just in time. Occasionally I even wet the bed, which revolted me. It was probably due to a reduced ability to control my sphincter muscles as well as the fact that I was, in order to fill myself up, drinking more than my shrunken stomach could hold. And as starvation results in delayed stomach emptying, I could no longer assume that if I used the toilet before going out or going to bed I would not need to 'spend a penny' (the sort I did not mind spending!) in a hurry later on.

Although I did not speak about these reactions, not even I could ignore them. Neither could I hide from the concern which my fading appearance was producing in other people. I thought that some people were exaggerating the situation in an attempt to persuade me to eat more, but I was forced to take note when neighbours who had not seen me for several months honestly failed to recognize me because such a change had occurred.

5

Imprisoned

I can count all my bones;
people stare and gloat over me.
(Psalm 22:17, NIV)

The Sovereign LORD has . . . sent me . . .
To announce release to captives
And freedom to those in prison.
(Isaiah 61:1, GNB)

By this time my G.P. had referred me to the nurse in the
practice, and I was going for a weekly 'weigh-in' at
which she checked my weight. I had increased the
amount which I was eating and consumed what the
nurse recommended, including 'build-up' supplements,
but I would never voluntarily eat anything additional. I
had not yet accepted that I was anorexic, and, because I
was still losing weight although eating what was
recommended, I convinced myself that there must be
some biological explanation for my weight loss. This
belief removed some of the immense guilt which I was
feeling. My G.P. arranged for me to see a consultant at
the diabetic clinic, Dr M., and I began to look forward
to this appointment. I even hoped that I would be found
to have diabetes, as it would be reassuring to know
what was actually wrong with me and I surely could not
be blamed for being diabetic. I hoped that when people
discovered that I was not starving myself, but rather had
a medical condition, they would stop giving the impression that I was a criminal or an idiot.

Before I saw the consultant I had to sit my higher

exams. The day my exams finished corresponded with my seventeenth birthday, and my parents had agreed to let me open my birthday presents after the last exam, as I wanted to have something to look forward to when I returned home. I arrived home ready for a little celebration, feeling relieved and happy, feelings which I had not known for a long time. My bliss was soon shattered when, to my dismay, I found my mother sobbing and proclaiming in near hysteria that I did not care about her at all, not even enough to open the presents she had bought for me. After calming down slightly she added that she had been to the doctor to obtain antidepressants because she was so upset about me, but she had not wanted me to know while I was concentrating on my exams. Going to my bedroom, I cried privately, furious with myself for causing my family so much suffering and being too self-centred to notice. I scratched and bit my body as a form of punishment, wanting to kill myself. It was the worst birthday surprise I have ever had.

Eventually the day came for me to see the consultant. My mother was with me during the whole appointment, and confirmed the fact that I had been eating reasonably well recently. However, I had already lost so much weight that although my eating had improved it did not meet my requirements, especially as I was still very active. Dr M. was naturally rather suspicious of me, knowing of the devious tendencies of anorexics. I stripped down to my underwear and she examined me. She called in another doctor to observe the fine line of hair down my back, a prime example of the 'lanugo' hair which anorexics commonly develop to give them some warmth. Many a medic was given the opportunity to examine my back in the months which followed. My mother later told me that this line of hair between my protruding shoulder blades made it look as though I was literally carrying a cross on my back.

As I was dressing again I heard Dr M. announce from the other side of the curtain, 'There's no doubt about it – it is anorexia nervosa.' For a moment I thought she must be referring to another patient, but when I heard my mother reply I knew that they were talking about me. I was stunned, motionless. It was as if a judge had sentenced me to prison when I was not aware that I was under trial. I felt sure that there must be some mistake, and yet there was nothing that I could do about it. I could not accept that I had anorexia nervosa, although the symptoms were blatant. A voice inside me cried, 'I am a Christian; how, then, can this be?' My definition of an anorexic was 'a stupid girl who wants to be thin and so puts her fingers down her throat to make herself sick', and I did not fit the description, as I neither wanted to be thinner (although I had a fear of getting fat) nor made myself sick.

My mother gave permission for me to go into hospital in four days' time. I told myself that when I got there and the medical staff saw the large (in my eyes) meals which I was eating, they would realize that I could not have anorexia, would find out what was really the matter, and then would let me go home. Reassuring myself in this manner, I emerged from behind the curtain.

Telling other people that the doctor 'thought I had anorexia' was easier than I had expected it to be, because those I confided in showed no surprise. My guidance teacher at school said that I need inform the other staff only that I was going into hospital 'for tests'. I passed on this message, and begged my teachers to find work for me to take into hospital, although I was sure that I would not be there for long. I would perhaps miss four school days at the most, I reckoned. I filled my suitcase

41

with books to take with me and gave my parents instructions about where they could find my other books, so that they could bring them to me if I desired them. That done, I surrendered my freedom and entered Aberdeen Royal Infirmary. There was no anorexia unit, so I went into a general medical ward which, because it specialized in diabetic cases, was at least able to cope with special dietary requirements.

After arriving in the ward, receiving the customary interrogation and changing into my pyjamas, I decided to go and chat to the other patients. I wanted to cheer them up and to 'let my little light shine' in that dreary place. I had a real 'need' to feel helpful and needed. As I felt perfectly well, I had no intention of simply lying in bed. Besides, my mother had said to me that there must be a reason for this experience, suggesting that perhaps someone in the ward would become a Christian through my example. I was more than willing to believe that it was God's plan for me to be in the hospital, as I could not see any other reason for my taking up a bed when there were long waiting lists for admission into the ward. I considered myself to be healthy and very much alive, although some people thought that I was at death's door (as I discovered when I finally left the hospital and was greeted by the comment, 'Oh, you're back – we thought you were going to die!').

My visitations to the other patients were soon brought to an end when I was reprimanded severely for leaving my bed. Although I had not been informed previously, I now found out that I was supposed to be on 'bedrest'. So began six weeks of confinement to one bed. I was not even allowed to go to the toilet, but had to wait for a commode to be brought to me.

Denied the right to visit other patients, I once more withdrew into my books for solace. I did hear rumours that all my work was going to be confiscated, because I was using up too much 'mental energy'. Thankfully this did not happen; it would probably have driven me to despair.

I did not find it easy to work, as my studies were frequently disturbed by the hospital routine. Ward rounds were carried out by the doctors, beds were made, and temperature, pulse rate and blood pressure had to be taken. (Taking my blood pressure was not easy, as the strap had to be wrapped round and round my stick-like arm). During the first few days I even felt irritated about the interruptions caused by visiting times. I wanted only to be left alone to study, and I still compulsively recorded the amount of time I spent working each day. In addition I hated the thought that people were putting themselves out to visit me. My mother, father and brother visited almost daily, and often twice in one day. I knew that my mother had a one-hour uphill walk to reach the hospital; and my father broke up his busy day and endured the long hospital corridors, despite feelings of claustrophobia, in order to visit. I did not like being the cause of such inconvenience. However, after a few days, visiting time became the highlight of my day, and I began really to appreciate the love and kindness I was being shown. Only once did a visitor make me feel extremely uncomfortable, by approaching me with a stern look and the words, 'Well, Deborah, what do you think you are doing getting yourself into this state?' Even than I knew that she was saying this for my own good, because she cared.

Although in theory patients were allowed only two visitors at one time, in practice the nurses were very lenient, and sometimes eight or nine friends congregated around my bed. When this happened they tended to talk among themselves, and I could relax and listen instead of forcing myself to carry out a conversation, something which I found difficult.

I was given over a hundred cards during my eight weeks in hospital, as well as many bunches of flowers and other gifts. Although I felt unworthy of receiving them, and could not understand why people were being so generous to me, I was extremely touched by the gestures, and I wanted to get well in order to please my relatives and friends. I loved getting flowers from people's gardens, and felt less guilty about accepting these than gifts which had cost money. They brightened up the ward all day and disappeared at night to be looked forward to again the next morning. One patient who was allergic to flowers was given an artificial display, which, I was amused to see, was also removed every evening.

Right from the start I ate all that I was given by the hospital staff, not leaving anything on my plate, with the exception of butter which I scraped off my bread. The control of my food intake had suddenly been taken from me (although I could choose my main course from the hospital menu, and sometimes actually got what I had selected), and I felt quite relieved as it could no longer be my fault if I did not gain weight. Breakfast each morning consisted of porridge, then toast and butteries. For lunch and evening meal, I ate a special thick high-protein soup, a main course, and a high-protein pudding. These high-protein foods were made up with a high-calorie mixture such as Complan. I was sometimes expected to eat the soup out of the metal pan it arrived in, which made me feel quite at home, as I often ate from a saucepan. At least I did not finish my hospital meal by licking the last scraps of food off the pan or plate, as I did at home. Soup which arrived in the pan had the advantage of not being cold.

The pudding at lunchtime was invariably liquidized fruit and custard, which was also served to the 'little old ladies' of the ward. It was quite nice, although the desserts of the other patients looked more interesting. In the evening I was the only patient in the ward to receive soup and a dessert. This added to my sense of guilt as I ate, especially when other patients made comments about the extra food which I received. The evening sweet was always a tub of a creamy mousse-like substance, which appeared disguised in various colours. On one occasion I was given by mistake a mince pie and cream intended for someone in another ward. When I expressed my pleasure at this variation, and mentioned my dislike for the usual puddings, the ward sister promised to let the dietitian know of my preference. Unfortunately the usual 'slime' turned up again the next day and continued to arrive throughout the remainder of my hospital stay. It was nice to be treated in a humane manner from time to time, when a nurse or a doctor discussed my meals with me and asked me to suggest any changes I would like, but it was discouraging to find that this never resulted in any alterations being made.

In a slightly less humane manner, medical students were at times taken to gaze at the specimen anorexic, as if I were an animal in a zoo. Although I felt embarrassed, I did not really mind being treated as an object, because I thought that I was helping the students. But I did wish that someone would explain to me what was going on. Several times the doctor we called the 'vampire' took blood samples, which almost caused me to faint because I did not have much blood to spare; but I was never told why they were necessary or what the results were. On the one occasion that I did ask why blood was being taken I was told that it was needed because the last sample had been lost!

At one point I was asked if I would be willing to have my rate of metabolism measured. I was happy to oblige. Once again I was not told what the conclusion was, but

I found the experience interesting nevertheless. I was instructed to fast from ten o'clock in the evening. I was very thirsty that night as the ward was hot, but the staff on duty were uncertain as to whether or not I was permitted to drink water while fasting, and so forbade it. In fact, I discovered later that there was no reason to prevent me from taking water.

After watching everyone else eat their breakfast the following morning, I set off on my 'camping expedition'. A fast-walking research worker led me through the long corridors to the other end of the hospital. My legs felt a little shaky as I had not walked for so long. But there was plenty of time to rest when we reached our destination. I was zipped into a plastic tent where I was able to study in peace for two hours while the amount of oxygen which I took in and the carbon dioxide which I expired were recorded. Afterwards, callipers were used to measure my skin thickness. The poor researcher found it almost impossible to make a measurement on my arms, as they had no spare skin to measure! I sometimes thought myself that I looked a bit like a scrawny monkey, with no fat and with soft hair on my face and limbs, and so how I looked to other people is difficult to imagine. I found it hard to believe that I had once been called a beautiful baby, and would have been used in baby-care demonstrations if it had not been for the fact that my umbilical cord took a long time to detach itself.

Having my metabolic rate studied made a welcome change from the daily ward routine, although I was disappointed that I was not told what, if anything, was discovered. Perhaps the reason that very little was explained to me was that I was so undernourished it was thought I would be unable to concentrate during conversations or to take in any explanations. (In fact, I had just sat examinations in which I obtained the top grade for each of five highers and one extra O-grade, which suggests that my capacity to think was not as impaired as some people presumed.) In addition, the medical staff tended to be busy and over-worked, and unable to spend as much time talking as they might have liked. Most of them would probably not have understood my situation anyway, as I did not even understand it myself.

My parents did manage to glean little pieces of information, which they passed on to me. For example, they discovered that the nose-bleeds which I frequently experienced in hospital had not surprised the staff, and were probably hormonally caused and related in some way to my (missing) periods. My mother was also told that it was likely I would start menstruating again after I had maintained a weight of at least seven stones for several months. My parents also received some information which I would probably not have wanted to know. At one stage when my weight had reached a plateau they were informed that unless my weight started to rise again soon I would be given strong body-building steroids to take. In my opinion steroids were 'bad', addictive drugs, taken by disreputable athletes. I certainly would not have wanted to hear that I might have to use them, and as it turned out my weight started to go up again without this being necessary.

At first I was weighed daily. On my second day in the hospital my weight was just over five stones, which was even less than it had been the previous day. I could not comprehend why I was still losing weight, despite the hospital food and the bedrest. Eventually someone pointed out that on the day of my admission I had been weighed at a later time, when I would be expected to be heavier as body weight fluctuates over the course of a day. Thereafter, weighing always took place just after breakfast, and I was weighed in my pyjamas. After a few weeks the routine was modified so that I was weighed only every second day.

My weight rose gradually, often climbing and then reaching a plateau before rising again. My father, being a statistician, drew a graph of the progress. Following a behaviouristic technique I was given a set of target weights to aim for, at which certain privileges would be introduced. The incitements included getting up to eat at the table with other patients (instead of having my meals in bed); visiting the television lounge; going (accompanied) for walks inside and outside the hospital; and, at the seven-stone target, going home. The targets were set without any discussion with me. I was interested only in the last two rewards and, lying in bed weighing under six stones, they were like spots of light on a dark horizon, far in the distance. I could not see the point of a bribery system by which I was told, 'Put on weight and you will be allowed to . . .', because before it was introduced I was already eating all that the nurses gave me. I later recognized that it was wise not to discharge me until I weighed seven stones, but when I had gained only half a stone in five weeks I began to despair of ever getting home.

I also resented the fact that I was being compelled to gain weight. I argued that this was unfair discrimination, as fat people are not forced to go into hospital to lose weight. As I got heavier, I began to notice more and more thin people. I started showing concern for some of my skinny friends. This was partly due to my desire to save them from having to go through the treatment I was receiving. I knew that I would blame myself if they became anorexic. I had heard of outbreaks of anorexia occurring in schools, and I was genuinely afraid that I might be the cause of an epidemic in my school. My fears increased when I discovered that one of my friends had threatened to 'stop eating, like Debbie' if her mother did not let her have her way.

However, the anxiety I felt when I noticed slim people was not aroused solely by a wish to help other girls avoid the perils of anorexia. Although I would not have admitted it, it was also linked to a hidden sense of competition, and a slight jealousy that I was no longer special because of my thinness. I did not feel especially thin. I was amazed when I saw a photograph of myself taken just before I went into hospital, as I could hardly believe that the skeleton in the picture was myself. While I was on bedrest, my face, which was the only part of my body I could see in my mirror, had grown very round and full. The weight I was gaining had not yet re-distributed itself evenly over my body. My mother joked that I looked like a toffee-apple, with a chubby face and a stick-like body! At least my glasses were no longer so slack that they slid off my nose, although they still seemed large in comparison with the size of me. To some extent I felt able to hide from the outside world behind them.

I envied one slender nurse on the ward who weighed herself in front of me one day, and came to little more than seven stones. She had the freedom which I, confined to my bed, was longing for. I could not see why I had to be a patient and she did not. I was just thin, wasn't I? What I failed to grasp was that I was engulfed by anorexia and preoccupied with my weight, which I had been allowing to drop continually. My attitudes, and not just my shape, needed to change. And that would be a slow process.

Although at times I longed to be normal and well, part of me was scared of letting go of the anorexia, my coping mechanism which sheltered me from some of life's blows. Had I been asked, 'Do you *want* to get better?', my honest answer would sometimes have been

'Yes', sometimes 'No', and often a confused and ambivalent 'I don't know.'

As I watched summer passing outside, I felt as if I were in prison. The question which patients most frequently asked each other was, 'When are you going home?' After watching some patients leave, I commented in my diary as a reminder not to give up hope, 'You can get out alive!' I was distressed by the thought of how far behind I must be falling at school.

But after my second week in hospital the school holidays began. Because I was no longer missing lessons my desire for release lessened. I resigned myself to the prospect of a long stay, writing in my diary 'May his will be done', with less desire than I had had previously to speed matters up myself. It was only when the vacation was drawing to a close that I once more frantically wished to be free.

Like a prison inmate, I was regarded with great suspicion by the staff, which was upsetting. Thankfully, I was not always aware of the extent of the distrust. For example, I did not know that my parents had been told that the window beside my bed should not be opened in case I threw either food or myself outside. On the other hand, some nurses did confront me directly with their suspicions. I almost laughed when I was asked if I had been making myself sick; I had no idea how anyone could have done so unnoticed while on bedrest in a ward containing sixteen patients plus the staff! I was also asked if I was taking diuretics (drugs that rid the body of fluid), as my urine output was higher than my liquid intake almost every day, according to my fluid chart.

I was soon allowed to fill in the fluid chart myself, although I was told to get a nurse's signature every time I received a high-protein drink, to verify that I really was having my quota of at least four of these daily. Some of the nursing staff expected me to get the signature when I received the drink, while others insisted that there was no point in signing anything until I had finished it, and so I was sometimes told off for asking for the signature at the wrong time. It was difficult to keep everyone happy, especially as I was expected to have all these drinks in addition to the liquid soups and puddings and yet still restrict my fluid intake to 2,500 ml daily for some reason which was not explained to me. I guessed from experience that the reason was that if I drank a lot I would feel full up and less inclined to eat. As my compulsory liquids alone almost exceeded my daily fluid allowance, I could not always have the cool water which I would have liked to sip during the night in the hot ward.

Although I could tell that I was not trusted by the fact that my chart had to be signed, I really became aware of the suspicion with which I was surrounded when I was accused of something days after the alleged crime. When I was seen one mealtime handing my plate over for a top-up before finishing my first helping, one nurse thought that I was leaving food uneaten, rather than asking for more, and she later falsely accused me of not finishing my meals. The accusation upset me, and I decided not to bother taking second helpings any more because instead of being praised for making an effort I had been warned that even the domestics would be keeping an eye on me in future.

I was aware, though, that the nurses were not trying to make life miserable for me and were only doing their job. My mother thought that they might be deliberately attempting to provoke me to anger by their inconsistency, as a display of anger from me would have been a good sign. But if this was the intention, it did not succeed. I only got upset with myself, not angry with other people. I came to the conclusion that I must deserve the rather harsh treatment and the suspicion which I received, and my self-esteem sank about as low as it could go.

I probably merited being under special observation more than most of the other patients. Soon after the second-helping episode I began to be devious again, as I had been at home. I was willing to put on weight in order to get discharged, but I resented not being able to do it my own way, which would have been by eating more of the healthy meals I liked rather than by having snacks and horrible drinks. Although I drank the high-protein drinks because I realized they had some goodness in them, I never liked taking a drink called Fortical which I was also expected to have. According to the label on the bottle, Fortical was almost pure sugar. I sometimes felt physically sick after taking it. Finally, when I could face it no longer, I managed to dispose of it discreetly in various ways. The clear 'natural' version could be poured into my water jug before the jug was removed to be refilled. The blackcurrant flavour was a little more difficult to dispose of, until I realized that it was the same colour as the water I was given for cleaning my teeth. It was light pink, like the water my dentist provided for rinsing out my mouth. When I could no longer bear the taste of Fortical, I surreptitiously added it to this coloured liquid, and so got away without drinking it.

Every day I was supposed to have a snack in the middle of the morning and another during the afternoon. At first I accepted the hospital biscuits and cakes, although I felt awful about continuously eating. Then a friend gave me a box of biscuits, and I was given permission to eat these in place of the snacks provided. It was easy to get away with consuming only half a biscuit or less each time, leaving the remainder in the box. Moreover, in the evenings my mother offered to make me a sandwich so that I would not need to have a hospital sandwich prepared especially for me, as they often failed to arrive in the ward. Mum brought me a sandwich only once. The thick hunk of rubbery cheese was not an experience which I wished to repeat. Even the care with which she had placed a pickled onion in each of the holes did not make the snack look appetizing. I told mum not to bother bringing sandwiches in future. Instead I hid the bread and butter which came with my evening meal and ate this at supper-time, allowing the nurses to presume I was eating a sandwich from home, although I did not actually tell them so myself.

I was not just playing silly games, or deliberately rebelling instead of trying to get better. I found it very hard to eat all that I was expected to, but did not want to argue about it. In addition, I was experiencing severe stomach pains from the sudden drastic increase in my food intake. My tricks were partly an attempt to reduce the pain, and to some extent this worked. When I had fewer snacks, I had fewer pains. My mother explained that my stomach had probably shrunk and the discomfort was caused by it expanding again. I disliked the idea of my stomach getting bigger. With a small stomach I did not need to eat much before I was full up, but I was scared that I might always feel hungry and want to eat if my stomach increased in size. So I had at least two reasons for not wanting to eat too much: my fear and the pain.

Another method which I used to try to reduce the pain was to do a little exercise. As I had been shouted at by a staff nurse for merely swinging my legs over the side of the bed, I realized that if I was to get any exercise it must be done in secret. And so, when the curtains were drawn around the bed to enable me to wash in privacy, I would perform a few sit-ups or press-ups on the bed. For variety, I occasionally slipped off the bed and tried touching my toes. This was more risky as the curtain did not reach right to the ground and so I might have been seen to be standing. I always dropped something on the floor first, so that if anyone noticed my hands going up and down it would look like I was fumbling for whatever had been dropped.

I had never heard of such schemes before, but I have since been told about other methods of exercising while on bedrest. Even anorexics attached to drips for intravenous feeding have been known to get out of bed and run round and round the drip while no nurses are looking. Lying in bed all day becomes uncomfortable. I was given a sheepskin rug to lie on because my protruding bones made long periods of sitting or lying especially painful. Despite my attempts to exercise, I often felt stiff from lying still, and my muscles wasted away during the prolonged bedrest.

6

Waking

When I awake, I am still with you
(Psalm 139:18, NIV).

During my time in hospital my father and my brother went away on a holiday which had been booked prior to my hospital admission. I did miss them while they were away. I could not get over the fact that they sent me a postcard every single day of their holiday. The day after they left, as visiting time approached and I knew that I would not see them, I was not able to hold back my tears. The nursing staff told my mother that this was a turning point for me, as it was the first time I had shown any emotion in the ward. It seemed that I was beginning to *feel* again, after shutting out all emotions, both positive and negative, from my self-centred cell of anorexia.

For as long as I could remember I had tried to hide any sign of unhappiness or pain. I have been told that I did not even cry when my head was cracked open when I was one year old. I had cried very little as a baby, and had often been left in my pram for long periods as my mother decided there was no need to pick me up. As I grew older I was expected to continue in the same contented manner. At an early age I had come to the conclusion that it would be wrong for me to look miserable or to seek sympathy, as that would indicate that I was not grateful for all that I had. But with my anorexia came a new development, as my feelings were not only hidden from other people but also became to a large extent unnoticed by myself. Although I could feel a tremendous sense of shame and guilt, and I was sometimes scared and very unhappy, I often felt no emotions at all. The starving brain reduces its expenditure of energy on emotions because they are not necessary for existence. When I started to awaken to feelings again, it was a somewhat painful experience, like returning to life after being in a coma bordering on death. The realization that life was going to continue, and the loss of the 'high' produced by undernutrition, were changes which were not always welcome.

While my father and brother were on holiday, my sister came up from Birmingham to keep my mother company. It was lovely to see Heather again, and I was grateful for her prayers for me. The medical staff, on the other hand, did not know quite what to make of her enthusiasm for the Christian faith when she came into the ward singing choruses. The day before Heather left again, she asked if she could wash my feet as a symbolic gesture of her concern for me. I had no objection to this request, but the nurses seemed rather suspicious, and pointed out that I had already had a wash. Not wanting to cause any trouble, I asked Heather to forget the idea; but she would not give up until she was given the basin of water which she wanted. We were told that we must not pull the curtains around the bed. I do not know what the nurses imagined we might do if we were out of sight. Perhaps they were afraid that we might change places, as we looked similar, and I could have escaped while Heather took my place on the bed!

Although touched by Heather's wish to wash my feet, I was not ready to accept all such gestures. My mother once offered to bring some rolls and Ribena when she next came to visit, so that we could share a communion meal together. I recoiled at the thought of having extra food and turned down the offer. Visiting time was a safe food-free zone, and I wanted it to remain that way. In any case, a 'service' with just my mother and myself would hardly have felt like communion.

The hospital chaplain's assistant did come and pray with me at times, and I was always very pleased to see her. Her gentle smile helped me to relax, and I was able to forget my own situation for a short time while we prayed together for other patients. My own minister also visited. Even so, I did miss attending church, and I considered it rather inhumane and unethical that I was denied the right to be wheeled to the hospital chapel once a week. For consolation, my parents bought me a personal stereo so that I could listen through headphones to a tape recording of the service at the church which I usually attended. I tried to listen to the service of the previous week every Sunday at the time when the next service was taking place, so that I could feel that I was with the congregation in spirit. I was also able to use headphones provided by the hospital to listen to the radio, and I was pleasantly surprised one evening when a request was played for me on the hospital radio programme, thanks to some of my friends.

The personal stereo was a useful gift. I also received more playful presents, including three little teddy-bears – to the amazement of my parents, who commented that they were rather childish for a seventeen-year-old. One patient in the ward, who liked to sit at my bedside and chat, became rather attached to one of the three bears. She named him Honey Bear, because she insisted that he was going to help me gain weight. Such conversations did help me see that life need not always be too serious! This patient was very friendly, and I did not resent her telling me that she would bully me to make me put on weight, and commanding me to 'think fat'. I was amused when she appeared for a natter even in the middle of the night.

The nurses could also be quite entertaining. During my stay in the ward I saw them having wheelchair races, skipping with the cords attached to oxygen masks, squirting each other with disinfectant, and leaving a colleague hanging in the air after demonstrating how to use the bath hoist. With such company I certainly did not mind being denied the privilege of watching television.

On the other hand, I did look forward to the time when I would be allowed to leave my bed. Occasionally it happened that all the nurses were out of the ward, attending the change-over meeting where a report on the patients was given before the new shift took over. I felt in a complete turmoil if a patient needed assistance during this time and there was no-one to give it. When this happened I longed to get out of bed and fetch aid, but I was afraid of the consequences of doing so and could only stay and pray until a nurse returned. Being confined to bed was very frustrating at such times. I also felt dependent and helpless when I had to wait for somebody to bring me water to wash with or anything else which I wanted. I had to learn to be a patient patient.

As I got to know patients who were very ill and yet desired to live, I wondered why I wanted to die, and began to rebuke myself for my attitude. After all, God had given me the gift of life, and I ought to be thankful for it. I told myself that I was wasting my potential and my talents by not eating properly and by lying around in hospital. The will to live demonstrated by some of the other patients eventually began to rub off on me. One patient who particularly helped me in this way was a girl named Heather who was only a year older than myself. Heather had been partially paralysed by a stroke, and had to undergo a five-hour heart operation which she had only a 50% chance of surviving. I was very impressed by her courage and determination, and her ability to remain cheerful. She was well loved on the ward, and we were all thrilled when she began to make a few tentative steps out of her wheelchair. Heather was in the bed next to me, and nurses occasionally mixed up our names. I laughed about this, as I had often been mistaken for my sister Heather before but had not expected to be called by the same name in hospital. No wonder I found it difficult to establish my own identity! Heather (the patient) passed more on to me than her name. Her desire to live was rather contagious, and it also began to spread to me.

7

Finding my feet

*I will lead them back to the mountains and the
streams of Israel and will feed them in pleasant
pastures (Ezekiel 34:13, GNB).*

*I praise you because I am fearfully and wonderfully
made (Psalm 139:14, NIV).*

By the end of my sixth week in hospital my weight had
risen to 6st 3lbs, the target at which the bedrest restric-
tion was removed. The morning on which I was
granted permission to venture out of bed I walked
rather unsteadily but very gladly towards the wash-
room. It felt wonderful to be able to walk up and down
the ward, talking with other patients, although I was
told off if I moved about too much. I have never
enjoyed a bath more than the first one which I took after
having to make do with basins of water for washing for
six weeks! I was also pleased when a few days later I was
allowed to leave the ward, although the excursions into
the fresh air which I had spent weeks thinking about
were in fact usually rather short. This was because the
nurses let me go outside only when visitors were with
me, and I was always reluctant to go far during the
visiting hour in case another visitor arrived while I was
gone and found only an empty bed.

As my weight headed for the seven-stone target at
which I had been promised release, I realized that if I
was discharged soon I might be able to have a short
holiday with my grandparents before returning to
school. I began to eat more and more, just so that I
could get out of hospital. I intended to cut back on food

immediately after getting home, although I was afraid that I might find it difficult to do so and be unable to master my appetite again.

On my last morning in hospital I worked my way through three bowls of porridge as well as the usual butteries and toast, and I would have taken more if a nurse had not stopped me. I also drank a whole jug of water, ate some fruit which I had been given, and tried desperately to hold everything in until I had been weighed. I sat on the scales trembling in anticipation. The previous day I had touched seven stones, the nurses had congratulated me, and I had rejoiced as I packed my bags to go home. Then Dr M. had appeared on the scene and weighed me on a second set of scales to confirm the reading. She then announced that I must maintain the weight for a day before I could leave. Although one day may not seem long in comparison with the eight weeks which I had already spent in the ward, the decision left me feeling depressed and betrayed. I had been told that I would be discharged as soon as I reached seven stones, but this promise was not being kept. The end of my hospital stay was in sight, but I could not pull it towards me. The following day I refused to build up my hopes again. Only after Dr M. had phoned my parents to ask them to collect me did I really believe that finally I was going to be discharged. Only then, when I was sure that I was not going to be weighed again just to check, did I breathe a sigh of relief . . . and discreetly head for the toilet to release the stomachful of fluid which I was carrying.

While waiting for my parents to collect me, I said good-bye to the other patients and gave my remaining plants to those who did not have any flowers. Even elderly Ina, who had occupied the bed opposite mine throughout my hospital stay, wished me well. Ina had great difficulty in speaking, and the few sentences which she managed to produce meant a great deal to me. I just had time to say my farewells to the shift on duty, and to give them a thank-you present (chocolates!), before my mother and father appeared, looking almost as excited as I was that I was being discharged.

I was really thrilled to get home, although a slight damper was put on the celebration when I discovered at lunchtime that my mother expected me to continue having the same sort of meals which I had eaten in hospital. I did not mind the soup and the main course, but when I discovered that mum had tried to imitate the slime pudding my spirits fell. Having been faced with this dish almost every day for eight weeks I felt that I was not getting my just desserts when it followed me home! Thankfully mum's enthusiasm soon wore off, and I slipped back into eating the same meals as the rest of the family.

Before returning to school, I was able to go with my mother to visit my grandparents for a week. Although mum had been warned that this was not advisable as I might lose weight again, the restful time in sunny Hampshire did us both good. After the holiday, I became a hospital outpatient. I had an appointment each week with a social worker who spoke with me and also checked my weight. I had been introduced to the social worker and a clinical psychologist while I was in hospital, but the two times we had met there had not been very productive. We seemed to spend most of the time discussing why I had eaten only half a 'chocolate bunny' (given to me by a friend) at one time, instead of the whole thing. I found subsequent sessions with my social worker more helpful, as we tried to get to the roots of my insecurity and unhappiness, instead of concentrating solely on my eating behaviour.

Certain themes kept recurring when I talked with the social worker, or with a friend who was a doctor. They drew attention to my unwillingness to show emotions ('bottling them up' instead), and to my lack of interest in the opposite sex. They also wanted me to identify problems in my life, and to find out for myself 'what makes Deborah tick'. For my own part, I was not sure if I was 'ticking' at all, and I wrote in my diary while I was in hospital, 'I wonder what does make me tick? Perhaps I've run down!' I did not even know who Deborah was, let alone what made her tick. My self-image was largely moulded by other people, based on what I perceived to be their opinion of me. This helped to explain my perfectionist tendencies, as I felt I had worth only if I achieved, and could not be valued just for being me. But I did not want to tell anyone about my confusion.

We also had two 'family consultations', when my parents and my brother joined the social worker, the clinical psychologist and myself. At the first meeting, as my sister could not be there, the psychologist asked us to imagine what Heather would be doing had she been with us. Fraser immediately replied, 'She would be sitting in the corner saying "Hallelujah!"' When Heather had come to visit me in hospital, Dr M. had referred to her as 'the missing link', the piece which had been missing in the jigsaw she had been attempting to put together. Dr M. believed that Heather might well have been anorexic too had she been living alone and not in a Christian community. As it was, Heather was noticeably slim, took part in fasts, and showed considerable interest in food and cooking.

When Heather had decided to live in a house with about twenty other Christians of various ages, my father had felt somewhat rejected as she now had a new 'family', and did not often return home. The clinical psychologist realized that I was afraid of the fragmentation of our family. I was secretly scared that my parents might get divorced. This fear had been reinforced on the day of their twenty-fifth wedding anniversary, when my father had claimed that the only reason that he had not sought divorce was that he could not be bothered with all the fuss, while my mother had retaliated by saying that she only put up with the marriage as divorce proceedings were a waste of money. This is not quite what one expects to hear on a silver anniversary, especially as it was said without a smile on either side. My psychologist thought that I might have subconsciously realized that it could take a crisis such as my illness to bring my parents closer together.

During the second family consultation the social worker took me to be weighed while the psychologist spoke with my parents and brother. I was surprised when I later learned what had gone on in that room, especially as I had considered one of the aims of family therapy to be encouraging mutual honesty and openness within the family, establishing an atmosphere of support and trust in which problems could be aired and dealt with. In reality, however, the psychologist, behind my back, had advised my parents to 'spy on me'. For instance, she told them to listen in case I was jogging in the bathroom (although with a bathroom as small as ours swimming in the bath would have been equally likely). Confronting me with suspicions might have had good results in the long run, but instead deceit was used to defeat deceit.

My parents rejected the offer of a third family consultation, as we did not as a family consider them to be of much use. We did not particularly like being told that our family dynamics could be improved. My mother read that weight loss attributed to anorexia nervosa has sometimes in fact been caused by zinc deficiency. She obtained zinc supplements for me, hoping that these would be more effective than the family consultations. I was glad that we were not going to have any more family meetings, as I could tell that they made my mother feel guilty. During the first meeting she had cried, blaming herself for my condition, and I found this hard to bear. I tried to comfort her and to reassure her that it was not her fault that I had anorexia.

I stopped attending my individual appointments as soon as my social worker said that she was happy with my progress, which occurred ten weeks after I had been discharged from hospital. She even added that she did not believe I had experienced anorexia nervosa at all. I had continued to put on weight during these ten weeks, on the whole, although there had been ups and downs. I continued to see my consultant about once every month, until one month when she was on holiday. Then the consultant whom I saw in her absence decided to discharge me, as he wanted me to put my eating disorder behind me and not have it hanging over me as I prepared to go to university. I felt gratified by the faith which he showed in me when he told me to throw away my Maxijul food supplement and return to a normal lifestyle, although he added that I could resume contact with the clinic if ever I felt I needed help again. I told him that I did not want to waste the Maxijul, but would finish the container that remained, and not replace it with any more.

At home everything did not return to exactly the way it had been prior to my time in hospital, because as a family we had decided to implement changes. We attempted to incorporate into our family lifestyle some of the ideas which had arisen during the consultations. In particular, it had been suggested that my mother and I should try to do more things together. Fraser and dad had season tickets for football matches and went to support the Aberdeen team together each week, but other than that we each tended to live separate lives, spending little time with the other family members.

Mum and I decided to spend more time together, although the ideas suggested to us in the family meeting, such as joining a sewing club, did not appeal to either of us. We went shopping for clothes together once, as the psychologist had thought this would be a good idea, but we both disliked the experience and decided not to repeat it. We were shocked by the prices and came back without making any purchases at all.

We also followed the guidance given concerning our family eating habits, and tried to have a family meal once a week. Although my father said he thought that the whole purpose of this was to ensure that I was eating properly, my mother and I believed that family meals had been suggested so that we would spend more time with one another and problems could be raised and discussed with everyone present. Mum had heard that letting emotions out is supposed to be therapeutic, and so she even tried to create arguments at mealtimes to encourage us to show our feelings. In fact, the arguments took away my appetite and made my stomach churn, hindering digestion. I was especially upset when the conflict centred on my 'picking at my food', taking a long time over my meal. Thankfully my parents had the wisdom not to make food into a big issue, although my eating behaviour was monitored.

Keeping an eye on me was not unjustified, because my tricks and deceitfulness did not vanish as I gained weight. I never wanted to be called an anorexic again, agreeing with my father that although a one-off problem could be labelled a 'developmental hiccup', if there was a relapse it would look like I might have a long-term problem with anorexia. Because my weight was still being monitored I did not want to lose weight; but neither did I wish to rise above the seven-stone level which I had reached. I still felt guilty when I ate normal amounts and I could not meet all of my mother's expectations concerning my meals. I continued to drink hot water with my food, but because this annoyed my mother I would hide the cup on the window-sill behind the curtain.

Changing my lifestyle could happen only gradually, one step at a time, but I felt that those around me did not understand this. I also felt unhappy about the restrictions which were still preventing me from taking full control of my life. For instance, my mother had forbidden me to go up and down the stairs to my bedroom more than a few times each day, saying that I wasted ten calories every time I ascended the fifteen steps. Although I had no desire to spend all day running up and down stairs, I did feel frustrated when I wanted to fetch something but knew that I was not supposed to do so. Instead of behaving like a stereotypical teenager and outwardly rebelling, I felt guilty for wanting to disobey my mother and more guilty when I did secretly disobey, which happened frequently. I became increasingly determined to give some evidence of a weight gain, so that the intolerable restrictions on my actions would be lifted. Consequently, on my weekly weigh days I drank as much water as I could manage before waddling off to the clinic. This had the desired effect, as it looked as if I was putting on weight faster than was really the case. My mother thought that I was doing well, and so was willing to allow me more freedom. She tried to motivate me to eat even more by donating one pound to Christian Aid for every pound of weight which I put on. She even said that she wished she could give me some of her own flesh, as she wanted to lose weight and I needed to gain it. She was so happy when she thought that my weight was going up that my cheating seemed to me to be justified.

It took me a long time to reach the point at which I wanted to eat and to gain weight for my own sake, and not only to please other people. Until I reached this stage I rarely or never ate a snack which nobody else would know about. I ate only because I knew that others expected and wanted me to do so. My whole life seemed to some extent to be a projection of other people's wishes and hopes. When I began to find my own feet, I accepted that I held the responsibility for my own life. I even found that it could be a joy to do things just because I wanted to do them, not over-concerning myself with the impression I gave other people.

Initially I managed to eat alone only by reminding myself that God saw what I was doing, and that although consuming food might not look like a praise-worthy task to anybody else, God knew where I was coming from and just how difficult apparently simple tasks could be. Gradually I began to enjoy food once more, and to thank God sincerely for providing it. I was glad that I was growing strong enough to be of some use, not restricting my abilities (both physical and mental) by limiting my nourishment. After all, a five-and-a-half-stone wimp is perhaps not the best candidate for missionary service in Africa! As I started to see that God loves to give good gifts, and I had been refusing to accept what he was offering me, the feelings of guilt about eating slowly subsided. Mealtimes became habitual parts of the daily routine, no longer laden with emotion and dominating the day. This process took place over more than a year, and there were bad days as well as good ones, but with no targets imposed on me by others I was able to move on at my own pace.

8

Acceptance

Oh for the comfort, the inexpressible comfort, of feeling safe with a person (T. S. Eliot).

I wish you would tolerate me, even when I am a bit foolish. Please do! (2 Corinthians 11:1, GNB).

Although I lived for a long time in a web of deceit, I longed to have somebody I could confide in and discuss my contradictory feelings with; someone who could accept me as I was. I felt that I was a 'multi-storeyed' being, revealing to each individual I met only the storey within me which I thought they wanted to see, and not showing anyone the complete picture of the real me. I was afraid I would be rejected if I disclosed my true nature and my deceitful ways. I was reluctant to remove my mask as this would make me vulnerable; besides, I did not want to be a burden to anybody. And so I continued to hide my true self, feeling that only God could really understand me. I was aware that people often judge by what they see on the surface of a life, but God knows what is going on underneath: 'Man looks at the outward appearance, but the LORD looks at the heart' (1 Samuel 16:7, NIV). I was certainly glad that I had God to confess to and be honest with. It seemed almost too good to be true that he accepted me just as I was.

Like my namesake in the Old Testament, Deborah the prophetess, priestess and poetess who settled disputes and led men to war, I placed great value on my independence. However, I also knew that I could not exist in isolation. I felt misunderstood, and craved

71

understanding. It was with great relief that I found, through reading a few books, that some of my feelings were shared with other anorexics. Although slightly different factors had triggered the eating disorder for each person, there were also many similarities among the causal factors and the resulting behaviours and emotions. When I met someone else who had suffered from the condition, I felt that I had at last found somebody who understood my situation and could accept me. Nevertheless, I did not find it easy to reach out to ex-sufferers. Meeting someone who has recovered from an eating disorder can be frightening to the person who feels secure in her anorexia as the permanent element in a world of turmoil. Anorexia is serving a purpose for her, and she will be unwilling to give it up unless it is replaced by another way of coping.

For a while my whole identity seemed to be caught up in my eating disorder. It was the first thing which sprang to my mind, although not to my lips, when anyone said to me, 'Tell me a bit about yourself.' I wrestled with the question of why anorexia had taken hold of me. However, I eventually came to accept that only God really knew the reason why, and that there are many things which I shall never understand. I decided to stop questioning and to put my energy into using what I had gone through to help others, if this was possible.

Six months after leaving hospital, therefore, I agreed to appear in a local newspaper feature on anorexia. I had written a reply to an anorexic whose letter appealing for help had been printed in the paper. My response to her was personal, but it was sent via the newspaper office, where it aroused interest. It was as a result of this that a journalist approached me about appearing in the paper. I felt slightly uneasy about this because I believed that people who knew about my problem were already watching and judging me, and I was not sure that I wanted everyone in the city to have the chance to read about my situation. I was willing to be interviewed only because I hoped that I would be able to help other people. When the article was published I was pleasantly surprised to find that nearly all the comments which I received about it, including those from fellow school pupils, were positive ones. I had even been elected by my colleagues to be a school prefect, although I had considered that they would think me too ridiculous to receive any votes. Instead, I was being accepted for who I was now, and not mocked for what I had gone through.

In spite of this encouraging sign, it felt good to be able to make a fresh start in a new place four hundred miles from home when I left for university at the age of eighteen. In Aberdeen my past was well known and I had become rather tired of hearing kindly meant comments such as, 'You're looking well', or 'Are you eating better now?' At Keele University my history was unknown and I was just one new student among hundreds of other 'freshers', getting to know people and enjoying the novelty of living away from home.

Perhaps I stood out a little, because I was so polite that initially I thanked each lecturer for an interesting talk at the end of every lecture – something that was quite unheard of! But on the whole I was just one of the crowd, and no-one was evaluating my eating behaviour (although as a recovering anorexic needing to gain weight I did eat large portions, which sometimes raised a joke about my 'hollow legs' because I was still skinny). I was free to choose what I wanted to eat in a way I had not been at home, and I avoided the most 'fattening' dishes. It was over a year later before I could consume a cheesy pizza, or chips, or chocolate cake, or ice-cream without feeling uncomfortable. The mere thought of such foods would have repulsed me two years earlier when I even thought about the calories involved when I licked a stamp. There had certainly been a change.

My weight rose gradually. As I did not possess bathroom scales I noticed the change only when my clothes became too tight, or when I weighed myself at home during the holidays. I tried to see weight gain as a good thing, and congratulated myself when I became heavy enough to become a blood donor. This positive attitude, and being unable to watch daily fluctuations on the scales, helped me to maintain the weight.

At school I had occasionally found it difficult to concentrate because I was too concerned about how I was going to cope with the next meal. But by the time I went to university, eating and weight no longer seemed terribly important. Whereas before I had been pre-occupied with myself and with food, I now became more aware of the outside world. I joined the Overseas Students' Society (although Scotland did not quite qualify as being overseas), and my friends from other countries taught me about life in their cultures. I also became a founder member of Keele Action on Disability (KAD), a group concerned with meeting the needs of disabled people on campus.

Moving to a university so far from home was a risky step to take, as anorexia still had its grip on me and I could have slipped back into its icy clutches. This was especially true as some of the girls I shared a block with were strict dieters, and regularly took laxatives to undo the 'damage' caused by a meal. I could have succumbed to the pressure to join them, and once again have gone too far with a diet, had I not been sustained by the prayers and the support of friends and family. Many people who have experienced anorexia do relapse when they leave a familiar environment. Some people had

74

expressed concern that I was going to study so far from home, one friend stating outright that I should be going back into hospital (as my weight had dropped below seven stones again), and not starting at university. Thankfully, in my case the move worked out well. It was very fortunate that I was staying in a hall of residence where the charge for most of my meals was included in my fees. Had I needed to buy my own food, it is likely that I would have eaten considerably less than I did, as I did not like spending much money on myself. But as the meals were already paid for I ate as much as I was entitled to, and so learned what a normal meal consists of. Even so, at weekends, when food was not provided, I at first lived on food which I had saved from the meals provided during the week, to avoid having to buy food. However, by the time a self-catering system was introduced one year later I had established a relatively normal eating pattern which I was able to continue.

I valued the freedom and independence of university life. Although my parents had been entirely reasonable about allowing me to come home late at night, they always liked to know where I would be, how I would get back, and what time I expected to return. At university I was free to structure my time as I chose to, and I felt unbound, and in control. But even more important to me than this freedom were the acceptance and understanding which I found at Keele, especially within the Christian Union. During my second term I was asked to be a hall rep. for the CU, helping to lead Bible studies and prayer meetings within the hall of residence. Leading Bible studies forced me to think through my own beliefs more carefully, especially when we discussed such issues as other religions, healing, abortion, or spiritual gifts.

As a hall rep. I was available for people who wanted

someone to talk to. I felt immensely privileged when people came to share their sorrows or joys with me, wanting comfort or coffee. As people were willing to share their deepest feelings with me, I became more open myself, no longer presenting only a façade. At one time I had felt unable to join in when we had sung at church the chorus 'Let us open up ourselves to one another, without fear of being hurt or turned away'. I felt pleased when people were open with me and dropped their pretences. For instance, I felt more comfortable when invited for lunch with a student friend who did not tidy up before I came and whose flatmate stirred her tea with the frames of her spectacles and ate tomatoes out of a tin using her fingers, than I did when dining with people who were obviously trying to be polite rather than natural. But I was very reluctant to be 'real' in front of people myself, tending instead to act a part. It was not until I had lived at Keele for some time that I began to take off my mask and show my true self.

Through being accepted and appreciated for the person I was, I became more able not only to accept food, but also to accept myself. Although I had committed myself to God when I was twelve, I had at times wondered if I could really be a Christian, because I had anorexia. As a hall rep. I discovered that I was far from being the only Christian who had experienced a psychological problem. I realized that it is common for Christians to think that they are failures and to carry a burden of self-blame because they feel depressed, or have suffered a nervous breakdown, or cannot give up cigarettes or alcohol despite the damage to their bodies which is becoming evident. Alternatively, a Christian may feel guilty because she or he has an eating disorder (whether anorexia, bulimia or compulsive eating) or another deficient coping mechanism; or because she believes that she has myalgic encephalomyelitis (M.E.)

but her doctor has told her that he does not believe in it; or because she has homosexual tendencies. After meeting people in all of these situations, I was forced to reconsider the question which had plagued me when I had been diagnosed as anorexic: can a Christian do this?

The fact is that (despite the teaching of some) Christians are not exempt from physical illness or disability, or from the pressures that can lead to psychological problems such as eating disorders. Some of the greatest servants of God in the Bible battled against physical or emotional difficulties, including Paul with his 'thorn in the flesh' (2 Corinthians 12:7–9), and Elijah who was so depressed that he wanted to die (1 Kings 19).

One of the pressures on young people today (especially on girls) is to be slim and attractive. They learn that they are judged on their appearance. It is therefore understandable if they become self-conscious and unhappy with their bodies. For Christians, this can be compounded by a misunderstanding of 'dying to self', and by denying oneself and striving for perfection. How easily we forget that God accepts us just as we are. His love is unconditional; we don't have to be perfect in order to receive it. In fact, we need to realize that we will never be perfect in this life, and being good is not good enough because we can never be saved by our own works. This is what makes Christianity so wonderfully different from other religions. It was while we were still sinners that Christ died for us (Romans 5:8). If we accept the salvation he offers, we should demonstrate that we believe in his power to forgive, by forgiving ourselves and then forgiving and loving others. Hanging on to a burden of guilt suggests that we doubt that Christ's death is sufficient.

The Bible instructs us to aim for perfection, but the word translated 'perfection' really implies maturity (wholeness, completeness) and sanctification (being made holy) rather than sinlessness. Our faith should be in Christ's perfect performance, and not in our own achievements. With a childlike trust, we can say to the Lord, 'Nothing in my hands I bring, simply to Thy cross I cling.'

I had known all this in my head for a long time, but I had gone on striving. I had not grasped the fact that God created me as a 'human being', and not a 'human doing'.

Gradually I began to share my hidden emotions with my heavenly Father, pouring out my feelings like the psalmist, and crying out in agony as Jesus had done in the Garden of Gethsemane and on the cross. I asked God to help me handle my feelings in a way which would glorify him. I tried to ask what Jesus would have done in the situation which I was in, and to put J.O.Y. into practice – putting Jesus first, then Others, and then not neglecting Yourself. Yes, myself. I realized that I am significant because I am a child of God, and that I do not have to achieve anything to make myself worthwhile. I was able to sing, 'Jesus, take me *as I am.*'

This all took a long time, but slowly I began first and foremost to hunger and thirst after God, and not after human love. As I grew more secure in myself, what others thought about me became less important. I needed to repent of trying to make it on my own, of trusting in my own strategies more than in God. I needed to acknowledge God in all of my ways (Proverbs 3:6), instead of trying to use my own understanding to sort my life out. I became aware of the truth that 'There is a way that seems right to a man, but in the end it leads to death' (see Proverbs 14:12). I had been limiting God's work in me, thwarting my potential to work for him, by offering him a flawed sacrifice instead of my whole being. I started to rediscover my self-worth, security and significance in Christ, not in anorexia. I also began to experience Christian joy within (which is much more than just a 'charismatic smile'), and to realize that the Christian life is not about slavery to rules, but is true freedom to be yourself, and to experience 'life in all its fullness' (John 10:10). Jesus not only fasted, he also feasted, and said that his disciples did not need to fast and mourn because he, the Bridegroom, was with them. Jesus loved to give generously and extravagantly, and still wants to give blessings to his followers today. I started to see that life can be fun!

As areas of my life were put back into perspective (although there are many things which I shall never understand in this life), I began to see that God can turn what had looked like a stumbling-block into a stepping-stone. I even thanked God for all that he had allowed me to experience, feeling that it had been worth it if it had brought me one step closer to him.

9
Is recovery possible?

Do not worry about your life, what you will eat or drink . . . Is not life more important than food? (Matthew 6:25, NIV).

What does matter is being a new creature (Galatians 6:15, GNB).

I am sometimes asked if people can recover from anorexia. 'Recovery' is perhaps the wrong word to use, as it is unlikely that the anorexic will return to being the way she was before the onset of the condition. If she comes through the experience, she is more likely to emerge as a different person than to revert to her old self unchanged. If she can pull herself out of the spiral which has been dragging her further and further in, she is likely to find that after succeeding in her struggle she has more self-confidence, greater self-esteem, and perhaps also increased compassion for other people who are experiencing difficulties. The anorexic thinking patterns may re-emerge during times of stress, but it is possible to find different ways of reacting to them, not immediately cutting back on food when difficulties arise.

An anorexic who has put on weight is not necessarily free of the problem, and in my case it took a few years before I really felt that I had recovered. When my periods returned I took this as a sign that I had reached a reasonable weight, but months later I was still trying to work through the pain behind the anorexia. When I left the hospital I was full of self-hatred. It took a long time before this subsided, and even now there are still times when I feel an intense self-loathing. But I have learned to remind myself that I am made in God's image, and that to hate myself is to hate a person Jesus loves and died for. If God says that I am lovable, who am I to argue with him? When I accept that I am a new creation, cleansed and forgiven, then I can be set free from a preoccupation with myself, and can show love to others. But reaching this realization has been, and sometimes still is, a struggle.

While I was being treated as an outpatient the struggle was just really beginning. At one follow-up appointment my social worker enquired, 'What do you do to treat yourself, when you are pleased with yourself?' The spontaneous response which I could have given would have been to reply that I could never merit a treat and could think of no situation in which I had been pleased with myself; I would feel guilty if I ever indulged myself. I knew that my mother occasionally bought strawberries and cream if there was a celebration, but I, on the other hand, had to have a good reason even to buy a cheap, bruised apple for myself. Thinking that this would sound self-pitying, I refrained from giving any answer to the question. I wanted people to believe that I was well now, but in fact a lot of work still needed to be done before I would be able to live fully.

Although humility is a virtue, there is something wrong when an individual believes that, if we are all parts of one body, she must be the wart! I had forgotten that the church, the Bride of Christ, will be presented to God without spot or blemish. Humility does not mean saying that there is nothing good about you; rather, to be humble is to acknowledge that what you have has been given to you by God. But I tended to lose sight of my talents and to magnify my faults. Even at an interview, when I was asked, 'If you were a flower, what sort of flower would you be?' I had difficulty in stopping myself from saying, 'A weed.'

If a recovering anorexic is aware of some of the possible causal factors of her condition, she may need to replace bitterness with forgiveness and to change some of her attitudes before healing can occur. I thought that forgiveness was easy and had never been a problem for me, because if anyone wronged me I deserved it anyway, so I could not hold it against them. But denying that someone has hurt you is not forgiveness, it is distorting reality. True forgiveness is not about ignoring a hurt because 'I deserved it', but instead it takes place when you can say, 'Yes, they were cruel to me, but I am willing to forgive them.'

Dredging up the past is not always the best thing to do, but when someone is not functioning adequately it often is helpful to examine why this is. A clinical psychologist or some other professional can be a good person to help with this, and usually begins by increasing self-awareness. It is often easier to be open and honest with someone who is detached from the situation and so will not be hurt by the emotions and memories which you talk about. Some people have unfounded misgivings about psychology being occultic or New Age, but in fact a clinical psychologist's role is simply to help people who are having difficulty coping with life.

An anorexic may discover that forgiving herself for her faults is as necessary for her psychological well-being as forgiving others. Guilt can be responded to by either forgiveness or punishment. I knew that God had forgiven me for stealing when I was young, but I had been unable to forgive myself or to forget the incidents, and so I punished myself. More than ten years after shoplifting I sometimes still felt guilty when I entered a shop. Believing that I was a deceitful and wicked person did not help me to act in an honest and good way. Only when I was willing to accept that I could change and was able to let go of the past which was dragging me down could I let go of my deceitful ways, no longer seeing them as an integral part of me.

Another way in which I started to change was by growing in self-confidence. Learning to drive when I was seventeen helped in this process. I was terrified when I sat at the steering wheel, but I persevered although progress was slow. I did pass first time though, to my astonishment.

Just before my driving test, I took another step towards independence by taking a summer job at the delicatessen counter of a butcher's shop. I enjoyed the job, and developed my social skills as I talked with the customers. My mother was also glad that I got the job, as it meant that we could buy meat from the shop at a discount, and have for free items which were out of date.

My pursuit of health and wholeness involved not only gaining self-confidence and self-acceptance, but also being willing to lose some of the protection which anorexia had provided. An anorexic can in some sense withdraw from the harsh world of reality into a safe haven. Being anorexic, like being obese, can protect a girl from male attention and female jealousy, as a piece of skin and bones is seldom thought to be sexually attractive. Anorexics are often afraid of growing up. An anorexic can preserve the innocence of childhood, as menstruation ceases and she maintains a childlike figure instead of developing womanly curves. During recovery she needs to come to terms with her femininity, and move on from the child's view that all sexuality is bad.

Throughout my early years I had believed that good girls should have as little to do with boys as possible, and so I had tended to avoid talking to boys. I was teased about boys during childhood, and I came to the conclusion that having a boyfriend was 'wrong'. Even as a teenager I was not at all surprised when my sister took a vow of celibacy in the community which she had joined. In fact, I thought that this was a very good idea. As I expected perfection from myself I also had high expectations of other people. I knew that I would never find or be a perfect partner, and so I preferred to remain single. I was glad when my periods stopped, getting rid of an inconvenient reminder of my sexuality. I certainly did not mind being without the ability to reproduce, not only because I believed that no-one would ever marry me, but also because I felt that it would just be too cruel to be the channel by which a poor child was forced to enter this troubled world.

My feelings of disgust towards sexuality grew even stronger when I was eighteen and an exhibitionist crept up beside me in a park. I felt so full of revulsion and guilt that I did not mention the incident to anyone until five hours later, when I began to worry about what might happen if someone else was approached by the man. So I told my father, who phoned the police. A policeman informed him that some young children had just been scared by a man of the same description while playing in the park. I realized that this could have been avoided if I had not delayed contacting the police because I wanted to block out all thoughts of sexuality from my mind. This experience made me aware that I still had some of the thinking patterns of an anorexic which I needed to work through.

Around the same time as this my habit of reacting to stress by cutting down on food was also put to the test. While my parents and Fraser were in Norway on a summer holiday, and I was living in the house by myself, I received a late night phone-call telling me that a dearly loved aunt had just suffered a heart attack and died. Everyone had thought that she was perfectly well, and I was stunned by the news.

For the next few days I felt sickened and did not want to eat. My stomach felt like a heavy mountain cairn, another stone being thrown at it each time I thought it had settled. But I knew that it would be all too easy to fall back into the cold comfort of anorexia nervosa. And so, after praying for strength, I invited a group of friends around to watch a video, and I prepared some food for us all. With my friends around me I made myself eat, and I found that my appetite returned. Although I still felt very upset, I had found a new way of coping with my 'upsetness', and so had taken a step forward.

It was important that I discovered some appropriate ways of responding to pressure before I went to university, as I experienced some tough times there, although on the whole I really enjoyed being an undergraduate. I was studying for a joint honours degree in psychology and English. I liked both subjects, and advanced in self-understanding as well as in general knowledge, as my reading of psychology made me more aware of some of my own behaviours and coping mechanisms. In my study of English literature I often found myself identifying with isolated, self-effacing characters.

I worked hard, and at the end of my first year was sent a letter by the English Department congratulating me on my progress. My mother asked me why I had not received such recognition from the Psychology Department as well. But I was pleased rather than disappointed. I no longer depended on external motivators as I had done at school. I got satisfaction from learning, and worked for enjoyment and not just for praise. This was fortunate, as depending on others for evaluation is a cause of self-doubt, and often self-hatred. Moreover, one is much less likely to get very high marks and to be commended by staff at university than at school. I did not have to rely solely on the opinion of others to feel happy with my efforts, and so I was able to relax a bit and be content in my studies. Although I felt encouraged when I did get good marks, I was more concerned about living a life which brought glory to God. His approval was what really mattered, and I wanted to please him because I loved him, not because I had to obey him. On my wall I stuck the words: 'Whatever you do, work at it with all your heart, as though you were working for the Lord and not for men' (Colossians 3:23, GNB).

During my second year at university I started introducing myself as 'Debbie'. Previously I had always been 'Deborah', as my father disliked the abbreviated version of the name. At university, finding my own identity included choosing my own form of my name. Going against my parents' preference was a big decision for me, even although it would not affect them in the slightest as they were four hundred miles away. It seemed to symoblize the fact that I had now separated myself from them emotionally, although they were still extremely important to me.

At university I discovered that someone who has been anorexic can recover not only to the extent of eating normally, but can also deal with damaged emotions (including forgiving those who have hurt her in the past), grow in self-acceptance, and really start enjoying life. However, although I never returned to an anorexic stage I am aware that relapse is common during the months which follow treatment for anorexia, and going away from home can sometimes trigger this off. For someone who is determined to recover, moving away can be seen as an opportunity for a fresh start. But an individual who has felt pressurized into gaining weight which she does not want may view leaving home as a chance to lose weight unobserved.

There is also a risk that the anorexic will become bulimic (eating huge amounts and then purging), or will turn into a compulsive eater. In hospital I was conditioned to believe that I was only a 'good' person if I had a full stomach. Had I not been aware that this was a potential problem, I might have continually wanted to maintain the feeling of fullness which was associated with being 'good'. This was made even more likely by the fact that I found it difficult to know when I had eaten enough, as I was not used to interpreting the body signals which I was receiving. Reversing the saying, 'If a man wants to eat he must work', I reminded myself that 'If I want to work I must eat', because food gives me strength and I can concentrate better if I am not pre-occupied with visions of food and distracted by a rumbling stomach. I was determined to eat so that I would be able to study, but my eating habits were somewhat abnormal. For some time I lived on one large meal a day, taken at midday, as I found this easier to cope with than trying to eat three moderate meals. I often consumed several bowls of a comforting, easy-to-swallow 'mush', made by boiling up together porridge, bread and milk, or bran, fruit and pasta. Almost anything which was cheap, filling and unlikely to make me fat could be tossed into the pan. As I threw in whatever was available, I did not have to think about what I was going to have for my next meal.

I felt in control when I missed meals, but when I started to eat I did not know when to stop. I brushed my teeth after each meal, as I had discovered that I was unlikely to begin eating again soon afterwards if I did so. The toothpaste was like a full stop, signalling the end of a sequence. Eating just once each day, and choosing food which took little time to prepare, also had the

88

advantage of leaving me more time to study and do other things. But it prevented me from leading a normal lifestyle. Gradually I gave up the security of my one-meal routine, and found that I was able to cope with a more typical meal pattern, and even to enjoy eating with friends.

It is worth being aware of traps which can ensnare the recovering anorexic. Whether or not she moves away from home must be her own decision, but she should know that she is supported by her family. I certainly received a vast amount of support. Heather visited me once or twice a term, as she lived only forty miles away. My parents and my brother helped me too, keeping in touch and always welcoming me home at the end of the ten-week term. This support was very important to me, assisting me along the road to recovery.

10

From anorexia to Africa

*For we are God's workmanship, created in Christ
Jesus to do good works, which God prepared in
advance for us to do (Ephesians 2:10, NIV).*

*I may give away everything I have, and even give
up my body to be burnt – but if I have no love, this
does me no good (1 Corinthians 13:3, GNB).*

When I was ten years old, my school teacher asked
everyone in the class to write about what they thought
they would be doing ten years in the future. While the
other pupils scribbled away about being firemen, nurses
or teachers, I pictured myself in the role of a missionary.
I was not even a committed Christian at that stage, but I
wanted to think of an occupation which had at least four
syllables. 'Missionary' sounded a bit more exciting than
'forklift truck-driver' or 'lavatory attendant', which
were the other options I thought of! Lo and behold, at
twenty years of age I did spend my three-month summer vacation as a volunteer short-term missionary in
Swaziland, in southern Africa.

In Africa, I was aware that a lot of changes had taken
place in my life since I had spent my summer holiday in
hospital three years earlier. The road from starving in
Scotland to serving in Swaziland had been a long journey of ups and downs. Now I was able to look back and
see how much I had changed. Travelling alone to
another continent when I had never flown before was a
big adventure. I had to trust that everything would be
all right, and that I would manage to negotiate all the

necessary business at Heathrow airport. Going to Africa sounded quite dangerous to me. I really believed that I might never return. But I had a sense of peace about the whole venture, as I had been praying every day for over a year about the possibility of working overseas and I knew that many other people were also praying for me. God had opened the door for me to go to Africa. I had even received simultaneously the replies from the two organizations to which I had applied, although I had written to them weeks apart. Receiving the rejection and the acceptance at the same time seemed more than a coincidence to me; it appeared to confirm that God was in control of all the details.

I had expected to be teaching in a Swazi high school, but in fact my main role in the school turned out to be running a bookshop and library, and doing secretarial work including typing and duplicating with an old hand-wound machine, usually succeeding in getting more ink on myself than on the paper. I did do some teaching as well, instructing eighty pupils at a time in A-level English, with no books available for what I was attempting to teach. I had imagined that pupils in Africa would be eager to learn, but I found them generally as reluctant as teenagers in Britain. Nevertheless it was rewarding when, at the end of the lesson, they were able to repeat the main points which I had outlined. I was delighted when two of my pupils presented me with a giant cabbage one day – a step up from the old habit of bringing an 'apple for the teacher'.

Working in Africa was a wonderful experience. Swaziland is a beautiful, mountainous country, and I loved going for walks in the hills and admiring the view, although scrambling up steep slopes in a modest long skirt could be a bit of a struggle. (Females in Swaziland are not expected to wear trousers.) Walking was certainly preferable to swaying along the dirt roads in a bus. I discovered that a Swazi bus is never considered to be full, and the passengers can always be squeezed further back to allow room for more. Keeping one's balance on a bumpy journey can be difficult, and even when it was impossible to fall backwards because of the lack of space I found that I managed to fall sideways, once landing on a woman whose lap was already full of live chickens!

During my three months in Swaziland I was involved in a lot of different tasks and learned a great deal. Most of the time I shared a house with another missionary. At first I found it difficult to come to terms with the fact that we employed a woman to clean the house and wash our clothes for us once a week. I had never thought that I would have a 'maid'. Soon I discovered that she was more than happy to have this job, as it provided her with a living wage and she even seemed to enjoy the work.

I was also able to spend a few days with a Swazi family in their isolated homestead, living as they did without electricity or running water or any of the other facilities which I took so much for granted. I suddenly realized how rich and fulfilling a simple lifestyle can be, compared with life in the West where people are rarely satisfied with what they have, always wanting more and more.

The generosity of the Swazis was striking. Although they did not have a lot to spare, they willingly invited me to share their meals, and they gave me presents when I left. On my third day in Swaziland I was invited for lunch at the pastor's house. I was rather regretting having walked thirty kilometers in the mountains with the school pupils the previous day, as part of their equivalent of the Duke of Edinburgh's Award Scheme. My long flight had also taken a lot out of me, and I was understandably tired. Moreover, I had not fully adjusted to the high altitude. I suddenly felt dizzy and faint, as I had done a few times that day, and I dropped the plate of food which I was holding. I felt very ashamed, knowing that the family had paid a lot for the meal. But my hostess rushed to get me a fresh plate and to clear up the mess, without a murmur of complaint. Such hospitality was typical of the Swazis I met.

The only time when I did not feel welcome was when the youngest children in the Swazi homestead I visited screamed with terror on first seeing me. I was rather puzzled by this, until I was told that the only white people they had ever seen before were nurses who had given them injections at the clinic. Viewed in this light, their reaction seemed entirely reasonable. I might also have felt unwelcome in the school bookshop as the novel which I was asked for most frequently was *Debbie Go Home* by Alan Paton. Fortunately I knew that this could not be a hint, as the pupils were not aware of my first name.

The Swazi people were generous not only with their hospitality, but also in their words. However, I found their compliments hard to handle. When one of the Swazi teachers told me that her children thought I looked like a doll, I could only laugh and say that the dolls in my house had squashed noses, squint eyes and tangled hair! When Swazi males asked me to marry them, which happened several times, I again tried to answer with a laugh, knowing that bringing a white bride (and her dowry) into the family would mean a tremendous rise in status for them. I felt sorry that such racial prejudice existed that the men presumed my refusal was due to the fact that they were black.

Swaziland is one of the wealthier African countries, but the contrast between those who have much and those who have little is very apparent. Slimness is not seen as so desirable as it is in western countries, because food is not so readily available, and because fatness in a female is held to reflect status in her father or husband. Diagnosis of an eating disorder is virtually unknown among the Swazi people. Nevertheless, the nation is becoming more and more 'westernized', and the young people love to imitate American youth culture in particular. In the school in which I worked, some of the girls did express a desire to be thin, and several wore tight belts to highlight their slender waists.

Many Swazis are plump, as they eat a lot of maize-meal porridge because this is readily available at little cost. Even the babies are fed this, although it is not good for them. Girls are now taught the benefits of prolonged breast-feeding, instead of giving babies porridge before their stomachs are ready for it. Swazis enjoy feasting together, and everyone in the community is invited to the feast which follows a funeral or a wedding. I was involved with the preparations for one wedding feast, and saw more food being prepared there than I had ever seen before in my life, as we catered for an estimated one thousand guests. Carrying bathtubs of jelly to the school fridge, I encountered two whole cows hanging from the roof, killed for the feast. It was quite a celebration!

As I have mentioned, I spent some time living with a Swazi family. The instruction to 'Carry each other's burdens' (Galatians 6:2, NIV) took on a whole new meaning as I learned the best way of carrying firewood on my head. I never did get the knack of balancing a bucket of water on my head, though, and succeeded only in washing my hair. I had plenty of people to teach me, as there were at least ten children around the home and they could carry water with no difficulty. Surely Jesus' words were true when he said that no-one who leaves their home and family for his sake will fail to receive 'many times as much' (Luke 18:29–30) – I had left one sister and brother back in Britain, and gained many more in Swaziland.

While living with my Swazi family I was given porridge three times a day. It came with egg, fish, soup, pumpkin, warthog, or virtually anything else savoury, and was to be scooped up with the fingers of the right hand. I always kept a careful eye on other people while I ate, trying to learn their habits so that I did not cause offence. In Swaziland it is considered very rude to look people straight in the eye, and I found it difficult to get used to the habit of not looking at the person I was communicating with. Still, I tried my best to adapt to the local customs. I was also wary about trying out the SiSwati language, having heard about one missionary who wanted to say that he was 'tickled to death to be here', but in fact put over the message that he was dying from scratching himself! On the other hand, I felt that it was important to demonstrate that I cared enough for the Swazis to try to acquire a little of their language.

In several little ways my experience in hospital three years earlier had been good preparation for my time in Africa. Getting used to porridge was one way – I had been given porridge every day in hospital, although only for breakfast and not for every meal. Having gone without a bath for eight weeks in hospital, I did not mind the days in Swaziland when I could not bathe because there was a shortage of water. (But I did enjoy swimming in the 'Cuddle Puddle', a heated spa, from time to time.) In hospital I had to be patient, waiting for a commode or a basin to be brought to me; and patience was also necessary in Swaziland, especially when I had a lot of work to type up using the school electric typewriter and the electricity supply temporarily went off.

When I accompanied the African pupils on a week-long trip to Lesotho, I could not prepare for the activities each day as I would have liked to. Instructions tended to be given in SiSwati, and as my grasp of the language was minimal (if that!) I just had to wait to see what happened. The Swazis do not pay much attention to time or to planning ahead anyway (as I had already discovered when I observed that the usual practice in the school bookshop was to let stocks run out before ordering more), and they could not understand why I always wanted to know what had been planned for the future. Just as in hospital I had not been given all the details which I wanted to know about my condition, so also in Lesotho I had to do without knowing all the future plans. It was not worth getting frustrated about. I learned to take one day at a time, slowing down and spending time with people instead of pushing on from one task to another without a break. This was a valuable lesson for me to learn.

I did miss hearing sermons while I was in Swaziland, as the church services which I attended were in SiSwati, but once again I had experienced something similar in hospital. I was able to pray and study my Bible throughout the three-hour services, and sometimes the main points of the sermon were translated for me.

I did not experience a summer that year, it being winter in Swaziland. I did manage to get a slight suntan, as during the day it could get quite hot, even warmer than the stuffy hospital ward had been. The nights were cool and it was sometimes frosty early in the morning, as we were high up, but the afternoons were often sunny. Winter was over by the time I left Swaziland, and I stayed just long enough to see the result of the early spring rain. The whole country was transformed almost overnight, from a dry and barren land to one which was lush, green and fertile. The words of Isaiah 35:1–2 sprang to life: 'the wilderness . . . will burst into bloom' (NIV). This caused me to think about how my own life had changed. My change had

97

been much more gradual, but I too had moved on from a crippled existence to experience new growth in areas of my life, with the potential of producing fruit. I had once been willing to give away all that I had and die, but had not really known how to love. Now I was learning to love other people, and to care about people all over the world.

11

And now . . .

He helps us in all our troubles, so that we are able to help others who have all kinds of troubles, using the same help that we ourselves have received from God (2 Corinthians 1:4, GNB).

I used to collect caterpillars, feeling that I had something in common with these unattractive, barely noticeable creatures which can be trodden on without their making a sound. One of my favourite books was called *The Hungry Caterpillar*. Like a caterpillar, there came a stage in my life when I built a protective cocoon around myself, hiding away in a world of my own, a world of living death. Nobody could come near the real me, and the façade which could be seen, like a cocoon, bore little resemblance to what was going on beneath. The cocoon helped me feel more secure, but like a larva which has stayed in its chrysalis too long I was beginning to wither. When I sang the song 'If I were a butterfly, I'd thank you, Lord, for giving me wings', I could not sing with sincerity the line 'But I just thank you, Father, for making me me', because I could not accept the person I was, and would rather have been the butterfly.

Today, I really like butterflies. Whether plain Cabbage Whites or gorgeous Purple Emperors and Painted Ladies, whether tiny ones or the large specimens of Swaziland, they exhibit freedom, and all their minute details seem perfectly made. Pollinating flowers, they contribute to the creation of something beautiful. Although my name means 'honey bee', I am really more of a butterfly person. I believe that there are many people who, like me, need to learn that we can stop hiding in our cocoons and can emerge and experience the freedom of butterflies. But this is a gradual process. An emerging butterfly remains attached to its cocoon by shiny, sticky strands. Some well-meaning people are tempted to cut these strands when they see the insect struggling to break free. If they do so, the butterfly's wings will never gain the strength to fly. Similarly, the butterfly-person should not be forced out of her cocoon until she is ready herself. She may appreciate gentle encouragement, but should be allowed to take time to fight for herself. It is unhelpful to tell someone suffering from an eating disorder that because you have prayed with her she should be healed immediately. Although God can bring about instantaneous recovery, it is much more usual for healing to take time. It is hard to watch someone struggling with those sticky strands, but instead of trying to force her into an existence for which she is not yet prepared, it is best in the long term to allow her time, remembering that the effort will be worth it, because she will be able to fly.

Even after emerging, butterflies are fragile and should be handled with care. For a time I was unwilling to give myself to close relationships, because to be open means to be vulnerable. However, we can only truly live and can only experience personal growth when we are willing to be ourselves, and are able to give and to receive the love and affection for which we hunger. Suppressed problems can prevent us from reaching out to others by keeping us turned in on ourselves. But when the problems are dealt with, we can be free to love and care for others.

I pray that, like a butterfly, something positive will come from my cocoon experience. But I am aware that I shall never in this life be able to sit back and say that I have arrived at complete healing and wholeness. My butterfly analogy breaks down at this point because butterflies experience 'complete metamorphosis'. Although Christ totally transforms us, the change will not be complete until we reach heaven. Life on earth is more like the life-cycle of such insects as dragonflies, known as 'incomplete metamorphosis'. Throughout life's journey we should be growing and moving forward, little by little.

I have learned to accept my limitations and I no longer feel that I must always aim for perfection. However, I still set myself high goals and am still something of a perfectionist. I am more willing to treat myself than I used to be, but I continue to be quite strict with myself. For instance, I still tend to buy cheap food. This is perhaps excusable as bargain hunting is not unusual among students, and I am not as extreme as I was when I lived on yoghurt on toast, or porridge and Vitamin C tablets, which were the least expensive nutritious 'meals' I could think of.

Although I enjoy giving presents, I still do not like other people to spend money on me. Since my seventeenth birthday, the day on which I found out how much anxiety I was causing my mother, I have not wanted to celebrate my birthday. I have kept the date a secret, and to prevent friends from finding out I have hidden the cards sent by my family. At first I did this because I could see no reason for anyone to be glad about my birth. More recently the main reason for the secret has been that I do not want people to spend money on cards or presents for me. I am beginning to understand, however, that people *like* to give presents, and I have been learning to receive as well as to give. I have stopped my game of 'pass the parcel', the term I used to refer to my habit of trying to give away every gift which I received. I have been given surprise presents and anonymous gifts while at university, and have been very touched by this. Recently, on the day before my twenty-first birthday, a friend (who did not know about my birthday) bought me a lovely bunch of flowers to brighten up my room over the exam period. It was as if God was telling me that, as a child of the King, I am special in his sight and am cared for. God loves every individual, and wants each one to receive good gifts.

When I sat my final examinations at university I was pleased to discover that I was able to cope with the stress. I had wondered how I would manage to cope when a psychology lecturer reported that the students most severely handicapped by the pressure of finals are females in large departments (such as psychology and English at Keele), who live in study bedrooms rather than flats, and are from overseas. The forecast did not look too good, as I classed Scotland as practically over-seas and so I fitted this description entirely. However, when the exams did arrive they came and went quickly and without causing me much misery. I found myself turning to other people when I did feel a bit low, instead of withdrawing into myself as I had done during exam times at school. In return, when others came to me for support I did not see their visits as interruptions as I would have done once, but instead was glad to be able to offer whatever help I could.

When my brother was born and was ill, my mother prayed a prayer resembling that of Hannah before the birth of the prophet Samuel. Mum made a promise that if the child lived one of her children would become a doctor. This was perhaps an unwise vow, but it was made fervently by a mother in the unbearable situation of knowing that her child might be dying, and at such times one does not expect to find wisdom. It is hardly surprising that mum was pleased when, a few years later, a fortune-telling gipsy insisted on telling her that 'one of your children will wear a white coat'. Apart from believing fortune-telling to be wrong, I thought at the time that if I was the one expected to fulfill what had been said it would more likely be by a career as a lollipop-lady than as a doctor! Nevertheless, I am now hoping to become a doctor, although not the sort with a white coat that my mother had meant in her prayer. I am currently studying for a doctorate in psychology, carrying out research on eating disorders. I hope eventually to train as a clinical psychologist. (I am glad that this has as many syllables as 'lavatory attendant'; otherwise I might think my aspirations had dropped since childhood!) God alone knows what the future will hold for me, but it is likely that in the years ahead I shall be able to use something which I have learned through my experience with anorexia. And whatever good can come out of the experience, all the glory must go to God who brought me through it to the other side and provided the love for which I was hungry.

Part Two

Offering and finding help

12

How can friends help?

'A friend is someone who comes in when the whole world has gone out.'

People suffering from eating disorders such as anorexia and bulimia nervosa share many of the same characteristics: for example, perfectionism and a lack of trust in other people. They generally have feelings of ineffectiveness, guilt, self-hatred, low self-esteem and depression. The main difference between anorexics and bulimics is that all anorexics are severely underweight, but most bulimics are of normal weight.

'Bulimia' means 'ox hunger' or voracious appetite. The bulimic experiences episodes of binge eating, during which she rapidly eats a large amount of food, and feels unable to stop eating. It is as if she is trying to fill an inner emptiness. Afterwards she feels guilty and disgusted with herself. Like the anorexic she is afraid of becoming fat. To get rid of the food inside her and avoid weight gain she makes herself sick, or uses laxatives or strict dieting and exercise.

Some anorexics binge-eat and make themselves sick, like bulimics. Some bulimics go through periods of starving themselves. Many people swing from one condition to the other. Because anorexics and bulimics have a lot in common, I shall talk about both conditions in this part of the book.

I have sometimes been asked, 'How can I help my friend who has an eating disorder?' There is no easy answer to this, because each person is an individual, and needs a different type of help at different times. You can be there to support and listen to her, to challenge, to set an example, and to give information. Sometimes she may just want you to sit with her, so it helps if you feel comfortable with silence. Watch out for her non-verbal signals, and be aware of your own.

Whatever stage she is at, one of the best things you can do is to show that you accept her, care for her and can be trusted not to reveal to anyone else what she tells you in confidence. This is more important than pretending that you know all the answers. Spontaneous caring can be much more effective than an over-trained counsellor who tries to reach the client through a haze of techniques which get in the way. The sufferer will probably not care how much you know, until she knows how much you care. Many anorexics and bulimics long for a close relationship with someone they can trust, someone they mean something to. The female sufferer usually wants a woman to befriend her, although it can be helpful if both a male and a female come alongside her, so that she can learn to trust men and lose her shyness of them.

Befriending a woman with an eating disorder can be a big commitment and is not easy. Progress is slow, and patience is essential. Anorexia and bulimia are disorders which cause a personality change. Thus your formerly easy-going, cheerful, caring friend may seem to become self-centred, tell you lies and start to avoid company. If you accept this at face value and respond by ignoring her, she will feel deeply rejected and will hate herself. The alternative is to be willing to listen to her needs, and to continue to be available for her. Listening is a skill, requiring that you put aside your own concerns for a time and focus on what she is saying. She will speak through her actions as well as her words.

A carer can feel a failure if the sufferer has such a poor self-image, and so strong a conviction that she is unlovable, that she cannot accept the love which is offered. The anorexic or bulimic is likely to have felt rejected in the past. Many have been sexually abused as children, and in other cases the disorder was triggered off when a boyfriend left. It is common for the sufferer to push a carer to the limits to see if she really can be trusted to stick by her. The person with an eating disorder may be over-sensitive and crave total acceptance and unconditional love. Only God can truly give this, and you should not blame yourself if you cannot provide all that she is looking for. But you may be surprised at the changes which take place when she realizes that you do care. Just as a tightly closed flower opens up when it feels the sun's rays, so she will start to open and blossom when she feels your warmth and your love.

The most appropriate help to give depends on which stage the bulimic or anorexic is at. If she is severely underweight, she will need medical help. The part you can play at this stage is to visit her and reassure her.

If she is not in immediate medical danger, she may refuse to see a doctor. As a first step towards recovery she needs to come to the point of acknowledging that she has an eating disorder, and to want to change. When a sufferer is severely underweight but is unable to see that she is thin, it sometimes helps if she is shown a photograph of herself with other people. The picture can show her how frail and unhappy she looks to the outside world, however big and strong she may think she is.

If she is still at the stage of denying that she has a problem, you might be able to help her admit its existence if you can show your concern in a non-threatening way. Perhaps you can say simply, 'I care about you, I'm worried about you and I'd love to be able to help. Is there a problem?' If you have already known someone with an eating disorder, or have experienced one yourself, or have learned about them through books, you might like to tell her about your experience to demonstrate that you have some understanding and will not be completely surprised or unsympathetic if she admits to having difficulties in this area. You could lend her or buy her a relevant book or cassette, to help her see that she has the same symptoms which have been described by others.

It is likely that the sufferer will experience great relief in simply telling someone the truth about what she is going through, letting the things she has hidden away come to the surface. Keeping everything to herself can be such a strain that the sufferer feels as if a burden has been lifted from her when she finds someone to confide in. Be honest with her, and unless her life is in danger try not to do anything behind her back. Building up trust is essential if she is going to feel able to turn to you. You should always treat as confidential what she tells you in private. If you can show that you are trustworthy and really do care, she will turn to you when she is ready to do so.

An eating disorder can appear to 'take over' a patient's life, dominating in every area and guiding her decisions. She may have been forced to give up her studies or her job because of her eating pattern. But in spite of this, in many cases there is something which is even more important to the sufferer than her food and weight concerns. While I was in hospital I was able to write truthfully in my diary:

> In the book which mum lent me, it says that
> food control is central to an anorexic. How-
> ever, *God* is central in my life . . . My family
> and friends are also important to me . . . If

110

only I could die and be with Jesus, it would remove a lot of people's problems. I'm such a poor witness.

If I had not been a Christian I would probably have committed suicide, but as it was I had something to live for. Although I felt at times far from God, I knew that he was holding on to me and that even away from my family I was not alone. My relationship with God was of the utmost importance to me. When there is something which is of more importance to an anorexic or bulimic than her eating patterns and her weight, then this should be identified and she should be encouraged to recover because of her relationship with this person, or the possible achievement which she longs for, or whatever it is. If the sufferer can become involved with things unrelated to her eating disorder – perhaps new friendships or hobbies – and take a fresh look at her values and priorities, she may be able to break free.

People with bulimic tendencies tend to be more willing to seek help than anorexics, because anorexics fear that they will be forced to put on weight. Normal-weight bulimics do not expect that they will have to gain weight. Although they may be scared that their weight might go up when they stop purging, bulimics want to give up the binge-purge cycle and are more likely to be willing to risk a temporary rise in weight.

Even when the motivation is there, a lot of effort is necessary for an eating disorder to be overcome. A carer can help the sufferer to find reasons for persevering in her recovery, and for carrying on with life. The patient might be encouraged to write down the benefits of overcoming her eating disorder, and to refer to this list when feeling tempted to give up. Her list might include the following: recovery will bring improved concentration, relief from always worrying about food and weight, an end to the continual feelings of weakness and fatigue, reduced irritability and self-centredness, better general health, an end to the life of secrecy and deceit, and a chance to be fruitful and to fulfil her potential in life – life on this earth is too short to be sacrificed to an eating disorder. She deserves to be well, and her recovery will also make her loved ones happy.

If she has admitted her problem and is contemplating change but is unsure how to go about it, you may be able to help her become aware of the alternatives, by giving informed advice when she seeks it. Assuming that she is not a young child, you should not push her into any course of action, but should let her choose which path to take. You can then support her in her choice. If she is given a diet plan, you may be able to help her to keep to it. Give her the praise and encouragement she needs, especially when she is slipping and thinking about giving up. She may try to avoid you because she does not want you to see her failure, but it is important that you remain available to her.

Show her how pleased you are when she achieves her small targets, such as eating three slices of bread each day or eating at every meal-time regardless of her personal inclination. However, care should be taken that your relationship does not become centred around food. When I asked women with bulimia and anorexia what advice they would give to someone wanting to help an individual with an eating disorder, one of the most frequent replies which I received was, 'Don't push the food issue.' The anorexic or bulimic should be loved for the person she is. You may be able to help her to think about things which are not directly related to her food problems, so that she develops other interests and is able to reduce the amount of time which she spends thinking about food and weight. After all, she is more than a stomach!

If you live in the same house or flat as the sufferer, she

112

might really appreciate it if you let her have the kitchen to herself at times. She might need this for a while as she readjusts to eating normally, because she may feel unable to eat at all unless she can eat in her own way. She might feel embarrassed about how much she needs to eat, or she may not want you to see her 'safe' cheap meals which are the same day after day. In time, she will become more flexible.

Let her know that you really believe she can and will get better. Yet try not to talk about recovery until she is ready for this, and be aware that recovery is usually a slow process. If she is determined to get better, you might ask *her* what help or support she would like. She might try to reject help because she feels unworthy of it, so point out that you like to be with her and enjoy supporting her. She should be encouraged to make many friends she can trust and turn to, so that she does not feel abandoned if one supporter is unavailable. This is better than allowing her to become too dependent on you. You cannot make her better; she must accept responsibility herself. Although the Apostle Paul says that we should 'Carry each other's burdens', he adds, 'each one should carry his own load' (Galatians 6:2, 5, NIV). The patient must be motivated to work at getting better, and not expect someone else to solve all her problems for her. Try not to let her become trapped in the role of being a 'patient'. Even if you enjoy helping her, you should always make it clear that although you love and accept her as she is, you are looking forward to the time when she will be free from her eating disorder.

After she has made considerable progress, your role can be to encourage her to maintain the improvements which she has made in her lifestyle. Anorexics and bulimics tend to bottle up their feelings of anger or grief instead of expressing them. The consequence of this is that instead of feeling the emotion for a short time and getting rid of it, they store it inside them and develop symptoms of long-term grief or resentment.

Bingeing and starving both have anaesthetizing effects. When she gives up these strategies, feelings that have been suppressed will emerge. She may need support so that she is able to face these feelings instead of running away from them. You can encourage her to show her emotions – but be prepared, because she may then transfer on to you the anger she feels towards her parents, or blame you for 'making her fat'. This does not mean that you are inefficient as a helper. It is her illness which is making her angry, and you are actually doing her good by allowing her to vent that frustration.

There is evidence to suggest that when anger is held in, the brain is depleted of certain chemicals (seretonin and norepinephrine). This results in a loss of motivation and energy, sometimes leading to depression. To put it another way, anger which is buried alive eats away at the inside, destroying the spirit. Suppressed grief is also destructive. The woman who does not allow herself to cry does not get rid of the toxic substances which may be contained in emotional tears (as opposed to tears from eye irritation). If the recovering patient allows herself to cry when she feels upset, she will discover that far from doing her harm or going on for ever, crying leaves her with a sense of relief from the tension caused by inhibiting her emotions. Laughter is also a good medicine, so try to hold on to your sense of humour, too!

Once the recovering patient has worked through her basic problems, she will need to work at developing effective coping strategies to deal with future difficulties. Eating disorders are not simply about food or slimming, but are a means of saying something which she has not been able to express in any other way. She can be encouraged to discover what she is really craving for, and to acknowledge her real needs and her right to have these met. This can be done gradually, taking just one step at a time.

Bulimics who try to stop bingeing sometimes give up after one slip. Instead of congratulating themselves for the measure of success which they achieved and seeing the slip as merely a little break in their progress, they conclude that they have failed. They do not agree that it is better to try and fail than not to try at all. As a friend, you might be able to help her deal with slips in a more appropriate manner. By doing so you can help to prevent relapse from occurring. If she binges again, you can point out how far she has come, and that one slip does not equal failure. It is easier for an outsider to see change than for her to see it in herself.

She is likely to forget the positive steps which she has taken and to remember only her mistakes. If she writes down what she has eaten in a 'food diary' she can see how well she is doing. She might also become more determined to eat properly as she knows that her intake will be permanently recorded in the diary. She might want you to look at her diary, to increase her feeling of accountability. Encourage her to reward herself for her progress, and remind her of the gains which she has made. In time she will become less obsessed about her food intake and stop recording what she eats.

A relapse can be prevented if the sufferer identifies difficult situations which might trigger a binge or starvation period and plans in advance how she can deal with these situations. Such triggers typically include feeling guilty, angry or emotionally 'empty'; boredom; the stress of exams or illness; loneliness; unhappiness; or doing something badly. Some patients can see from their diaries the situations which have caused problems in the past. They can then think about new ways in which they can handle such situations. If the sufferer is not yet ready to confront the root cause of her anger or unhappiness, you can help her to work out a short-term strategy to deal with her feelings in a constructive manner. She can work on the root of the problem later.

A solution might be as basic as to phone you or another friend, or to go out of the house, perhaps going for a walk after a meal instead of sitting feeling miserable. You could encourage her to take a nap when she feels tired, instead of forcing herself to stay awake. She can be encouraged to say 'That makes me angry' when someone annoys her, instead of taking out her angry feelings on herself.

You might offer to keep her company when she feels down, or to do something with her in the evenings if that is when she is most tempted to binge. When she thinks she is going to lapse into the dream-like state of a binge, she can train herself to concentrate on the here-and-now, perhaps describing all of the things which she can see and hear (vase of yellow flowers, books on a shelf, necklace I was given by a friend, children laughing, birds singing . . .). Not only does this exercise make her thankful for what she has, but it also engages her awareness, and tends to forestall the loss of control which accompanies a binge.

The best 'distractor activities' vary from person to person, and it can be helpful if she draws up a list of things to do when feeling low, and if she works out in advance how she will cope with difficult occasions, such as parties. Christmas tends to be a very stressful time for people with eating disorders (and also for their families). With a house full of alcohol, Christmas cakes, mince pies, Christmas puddings, nuts, turkey and stuffing and all the rest of the festive foods, the bulimic has binge triggers on every side, while the anorexic is likely to be surrounded by relatives who are trying to make her eat. How will she survive such celebrations?

Many recovering bulimics and anorexics would rather have a meal with a trusted, reassuring friend than alone. This might be because they know that they will not binge when someone else is there, or because they feel that there is little point in having a meal if no-one else will know about it. A supporter can help the sufferer find new ways in which she can show her strength and will-power. Her self-esteem can be built up as she learns to make her views known, to be firmer with other people and to say 'No'. She can discover more appropriate areas in which she can achieve, so that she feels less need to exert extreme control over her weight. When she is made aware of her good points, she is less likely to see dieting as her sole strength and achievement. One five-and-a-half-stone anorexic recovered and became a champion female arm-wrestler!

It is good if the recovering patient has something to look forward to each day, to give her days some structure. Even a phone-call or a trip to the library can help to break up the monotony of a day. She should be encouraged to set herself goals, so that she has something to plan and get enthusiastic about which is unrelated to weight. Her plans might involve anything from making a church banner to fund raising for people in the Third World to having a holiday abroad. All of these activities will help her to become involved with other people again, and to build up a network of friends and broaden her horizons so that she is no longer concerned only with her own shrunken world.

It is also helpful if she can do things where she feels in control, whether drawing up a rota of people to help out at a group she attends, or looking after plants (or cats or babies, which she can cuddle as well as control; plants are not quite so cuddly!).

The sufferer should be advised not to make important

long-term decisions (such as deciding to move house) while she is in a state of turmoil, if this is possible. As she comes through the storm she may begin to make plans for her future, including choosing a profession if she does not already have one. If she is lacking in confidence she might need a lot of encouragement before she will apply for a job. Left to herself she is likely to accept a post far below her potential ability just so that she can be sure she will not fail in it. She should be encouraged to take a challenge. At times of high unemployment, when nearly all job-seekers have to cope with lots of rejection letters, your support will be particularly vital to her. When she does gain work, whether voluntary or paid, her self-esteem will be built up. If she can earn some money which is her own she may feel more effective, and more willing to spend money on herself.

You can also support the sufferer as she tries to get rid of unhealthy habits such as taking laxatives. She may feel reassured if you can tell her what to expect when she tries to end her reliance on laxatives, and if you encourage her as she goes about this. Ending any drug addiction is a big achievement, and praise should be given when she succeeds.

Reminding her that laxatives do not get rid of many extra calories can help to keep her motivation up. The only pounds that laxatives help you to lose are the pounds they cost to buy. Laxative abuse can have many unpleasant effects, including abdominal pain, dizziness, thirst, damage to the kidneys and the liver, and an imbalance of chemicals within the body which in extreme cases can cause a heart attack. Many people do manage to give up laxatives when they are made aware of the dangers. In one study, 62% of questionnaire respondents who had tried to come off laxatives reported that they had succeeded in doing so. They admitted that it had not been easy, but with perseverance they were successful.

When someone has been taking a lot of laxatives it is advisable to reduce the dosage gradually rather than suddenly deciding not to take any more. Otherwise it is likely not only that bowel movements will stop but that the effects of drug withdrawal known as 'cold turkey' will occur. People who experience 'cold turkey' tend to shake all over and find light and sound painful, because addictive drugs (including laxatives) often dull sensations. This means that when the effect of the drugs wears off, the individual suddenly becomes sensitive once more to factors in the environment.

It is best to avoid high-fibre foods (such as potatoes, wholemeal bread, bran cereals and baked beans) for the first few laxative-free weeks, to prevent painful feelings of cramps and bloating. At the same time, at least six glasses of water should be drunk each day. This helps the body to get rid of the excess fluid which it has retained while laxatives have been relied on. Although drinking in order to get rid of fluid sounds like a contradiction in terms, the body needs to realize that it is no longer necessary to store water, because enough fluid is being taken in. The body will then get rid of its store of water, and the 'bloated' feelings should disappear.

You can help the sufferer just by giving her information such as this. Information about eating disorders can help her to see that she is not alone. It can also help her to begin to talk. For instance, you might mention that it is common for people with eating disorders to have been abused in childhood. She then has the opportunity of talking about any abuse which she may have experienced, if she is ready to share this. The issue must be raised in a non-threatening manner, however.

If you are a Christian carer you can allow Jesus to work through you. When stuck for words you can ask,

'What would Jesus do in this situation?', pray for wisdom and act accordingly. Perhaps you can encourage the sufferer to try to do this too. When you really are lost for words, there is nothing wrong with being honest and saying, 'I don't know what to say.' After spending time with her, remember to pray and to hand the whole situation back over to God, so that the burden is not left on your shoulders. This is especially important if she is depressed, as depression can be contagious; or if she has been speaking about traumatic memories, such as past abuse, which might prey on your mind. Ask God to bring in his light for you.

This is important, because as you empathize with the sufferer, you may begin to be affected by her symptoms. For instance, listening to her talk about food, starving or bingeing may cause a temporary increase or decrease in your own appetite. You may even start to feel guilty about enjoying your food. You might start to notice how thin your friends are, and almost become obsessed with what they eat. Their talk about dieting may arouse strong feelings of anger in you, and leave you feeling lonely because you think they cannot understand the way you feel.

You might identify with the sufferer's feelings of powerlessness. Some mothers become over-anxious about their children or over-protective of them, after listening to someone with an eating disorder. If she has confided in you that she was abused or rejected as a child, you may lose trust in your own family or partner as you start to think that nothing is ever as it seems. None of this needs to happen. It will not occur as long as you are aware of the possibility and do not become so involved with the eating disorder situation or identify so much with the sufferer that you cannot see the world beyond.

If you are putting a lot of effort into helping people

with eating disorders, try to find someone who is interested in what you are doing and will listen to you, pray for you and encourage you. It is worth making the effort to contact other people who are doing similar work, as they are likely to understand your feelings, such as frustration, disappointment, perplexity when prayers seem unanswered, impatience or anger. They may also be able to offer fresh perspectives, and to share your joy when progress is made. Believe that your work is valuable, and spend time with friends who affirm the value of what you are doing and help you not to give up hope. You are carrying a heavy burden – the person you are helping could suddenly die – and so you will need support. If you become so drained that you feel inadequate and helpless, you are not doing anyone any favours, including the sufferer who will feel even more guilty when she realizes she has depleted her helper. Symptoms of stress are common among carers and do not mean that you are incompetent, but they may mean that you need to take more care of yourself. Remember that no person can remove all the sufferer's pain or fill all her emptiness. You are doing your best to help, but if she does not show signs of improvement, this is not your fault.

Although you want to help the person who is recovering from bulimia or anorexia, you should be willing to recognize your limitations, and you must remember that your own needs are important. If your friend keeps wanting to speak to you in the middle of the night, let her know that you will be better able to help her in the morning, and that you need to sleep. She may have become so caught up in her problem that she cannot see things from your angle at all, but if you explain your situation she is likely to understand. You must set boundaries, so that you do not completely burn out. Your example may help her to see how she can set limits in her relationships and can learn to say 'no', like you. She may possibly test you out or try to manipulate you, and if she does so you should speak to her honestly about how this makes you feel. Point out that what you are resisting is not her, but the manipulative behaviour which is a part of her illness.

When you feel out of your depth, let someone else help out, rather than trying to provide all the answers yourself. There is nothing wrong with admitting that you do not have all the answers, and that someone else may be better qualified to help. This does not mean that you are rejecting her – you are still there, but would like someone else to help too. After all, it is unlikely that you would offer to give a friend heart surgery if your only qualifications were a lot of compassion and a certificate in basic first aid. Sometimes therapy sessions can be as delicate as heart surgery.

If you have been remembering the sufferer during your private prayer times, you might want to pray *with* her. You should ask her first if she would like this, explaining that she does not need to pray out loud. You should also ask what she would like you to pray about, as she may not want complete healing at the moment but might desire, for instance, to experience peace and to be able to sleep. You can offer to pray about her future, about any painful relationships which she is involved in, and about feelings of grief or guilt which she may be experiencing. She might want you to pray that her body will be physically protected and healthy. You can also ask that God will enable her to see with his eyes, and that she will feel surrounded by his love and know her worth. A short and simple prayer, perhaps said while holding the sufferer's hands, can be very powerful.

If the patient is herself a Christian, but is finding it difficult to pray, your example can help her in her prayer life. The Christian life is stunted when bulimia or anorexia develop, because the sufferer feels that her eating pattern is bad and separates her from God. You can encourage her to pray at all times, including when she is in distress. God is a friend and a comforter, 'our refuge and strength, an ever present help in trouble' (Psalm 46:1, NIV). When we give praise to God, our eyes are lifted from our own weakness to his strength. You might also encourage her to read the Bible and to spend time with other Christians. It can help if you read a small Bible passage with her, and discuss what you have read, without forcing interpretations on to her.

It is good to invite a sufferer to become involved in a church if she does not already attend one, but you should not pressurize her into attending your particular church. Instead, help her to find the place that is right for her. If she has been abused, even talking a lot about 'Father God' and calling her 'sister' can make her panic, while she may be terrified by a church where she is greeted with a hug or kiss at the door. She might feel 'safer' in a large congregation, where she can remain anonymous, than in a small fellowship. Some sufferers find long, lively worship sessions full of 'hallelujahs' too much for them, and feel insecure and out of place in a large crowd of uninhibited worshippers. They prefer a quiet, predictable service where the 'still small voice of calm' can reassure them. We should be sensitive to people's different needs, and not expect everyone to be like us.

Some recovering anorexics and bulimics are very grateful for any practical help they are offered in re-establishing normal eating habits. They appreciate having a friend who will go shopping with them, and teach them about normal portion sizes – and help them to avoid automatically stocking up with binge foods.

At some stage you might feel that you would like to

invite the recovering patient for a meal. If you are unsure whether or not she can cope with this yet, make it clear that you will not be offended if she turns down the offer. If you give her a written invitation she will have time to think, instead of having to make an on-the-spot decision. If she accepts your offer, prepare a simple meal, as anything extravagant will make her feel guilty. She is likely to feel very self-conscious, so try to avoid watching her while she is eating. She will be able to see from your example what a 'normal meal' might be. She may even discover that eating can be an enjoyable and natural activity.

Some carers even consider 'adopting' a sufferer, inviting her to become part of their family and offering the love which she may have missed out on during childhood. This demonstrates that she is not unlovable and it is not her fault that life at home was difficult. When you have got to know each other and feel comfortable together, you could invite her to stay for a few days or longer. Having a recovering bulimic or anorexic in your house will put pressure on yourself and your family, and you should think carefully before deciding to take this step. But it can be exceedingly rewarding for the family, and life-changing for the sufferer. It is easier for her to break the fasting or binge-purge habit and to establish normal meal patterns when living in another home, away from the house or flat with which the old routine is associated.

Always be truthful with the sufferer. Be willing to admit that you have problems yourself, and to let people see the 'real you', so that the recovering sufferer does not feel such a failure because she has problems. You can even let *her* support *you* when you find the going tough. If you provide an example of self-disclosing openness, she may begin to open up and share her thoughts and feelings. If you are accepting of yourself, resenting neither your body nor your personality, then you are setting a good example. You should also be careful not to gossip, because if you talk about others behind their backs she will presume that you do the same about her, and will lose all faith in you.

As she becomes better and better, you should remain available to her, showing love and letting her know that she is a worthwhile person. Otherwise she may be reluctant to let go of her eating disorder because she thinks that people only care for her while she is ill, and will 'drop her' when things seem to have improved. Even when she appears to have overcome her eating problems, it is invaluable for her to know that there is a friend she can turn to at any time. On encountering fresh difficulties, as we all do on occasion, it is easier to talk to someone who has already stood by you through hard times than to try to explain yourself from scratch to a new person.

The Eating Disorders Association (EDA) may be able to answer any specific questions which you have. If you are willing to consider becoming a carer with Anorexia and Bulimia Care (ABC), or would like to receive more training concerning how to care for people with eating disorders, please contact ABC. These charities would also greatly appreciate any financial help which you can offer. The addresses are given at the back of the book.

You might also want to offer your support to the campaign PLAN (Prevent Laxative Abuse Now). Because laxatives have the potential to be abused, according to the pharmacists' code of practice they should be sold only in chemist shops and with the pharmacist's approval. But in fact they can be bought in many general shops, and even at petrol stations. PLAN supporters have been urging the manufacturers of laxatives to take measures to reduce the risk of these drugs being abused. Such measures include selling laxatives only in small packets and not in bulk, and printing on packets the warning that laxatives do not stop the body absorbing calories, and that taking more than the stated dose can have harmful effects. The address to contact for more information about the PLAN campaign is listed at the end of the book.

The good news is that the number of people suffering (and dying) from eating disorders does not need to continue to rise. There are preventative measures which can be taken to help reduce the likelihood of people developing eating disorders. One important means of lessening the risk of any developmental disorder emerging is to build up the self-esteem of young people, valuing them for who they are and not just for what they do. Young people (and older people as well) can also be taught coping strategies. Knowing how to cope with problem areas enhances the sense of self-control, confidence and self-esteem.

Where onlookers are able to detect signs of stress and the first symptoms of an eating disorder, support can be offered early enough to stop the progression of the condition, and to help the individual cope in a healthier way.

Teachers, especially those who teach matters related to health (in biology, cookery or physical education lessons) have the opportunity to teach the ill-effects of being too thin as well as the risks of being overweight. By challenging the assumption that 'one can never be too rich or too thin', over-dieting loses some of its attraction.

A growing number of people are becoming aware that anorexia and bulimia have been eating away at people in our society for too long. Where awareness and understanding are present, there is a lot of hope.

13

How can the church help?

The local church can be a wonderful source of help for someone who is passing through a difficult time, providing acceptance, love and support. At church the sufferer can meet people in a variety of situations, and may forget about her own difficulties for a time. Where there is understanding, she can receive great strength from her involvement with a church as well as from her personal relationship with Jesus, the head of the church.

Sometimes would-be comforters actually make us feel worse. Job (in the Old Testament) is not the only person to have discovered this. A sufferer told me that some churches should have a government health warning pinned on their noticeboards. One compulsive eater told me that after I had given a talk about eating disorders at her church, a male deacon came up to her and said as a joke, 'I think we both must suffer from these eating disorders, we are so huge!' She pretended to laugh, but actually the comment made her want to cry.

I know of at least one sufferer who felt humiliated and found it very hard to cope when she was called out to the front of a church and the congregation was told that she had received prayer and had 'been healed from anorexia'. In another church the congregation clapped when it was announced that an anorexic among them had gained a stone in weight. Sufferers feel very upset when treated in such ways. They are embarrassed about their eating disorder and very sensitive about their weight.

Sufferers are also uncomfortable when people expect them to receive spontaneous healing. Although immediate healings do sometimes occur, it is much more common for recovery to proceed slowly, step by step. The sufferer should be offered support as she makes progress, rather than be made to feel guilty for not being cured straight away. Nor should she be told in a judgmental way that her illness is 'sinful'. Although it is wrong to abuse the body, this is something we all do to some extent, whether by exercising too much or too little, over-eating or under-eating, getting too much sleep or not enough of it, having bad posture, and so on. Scratching oneself could be termed self-abuse, but few people would condemn someone for responding to an itch. An eating disorder is a reaction to an underlying 'itch'. None of us has the right to judge anyone else.

Cases where the patient feels humiliated by the church are thankfully uncommon. More often, people in a fellowship try to ignore the eating disorder because they do not know how they can help. Anorexia and Bulimia Care (ABC) offers advice and training to congregations wanting to find out more about eating disorders and how they can offer support. Unfortunately a lot of churches do not seem to want this information, even when an anorexic or bulimic in their midst has asked ABC to contact the church. Several sufferers have said to me that they really wish someone in their fellowship had an understanding of eating disorders. One bulimic stated that when she does not go to church, people within the congregation assume that this is because she is not really committed, instead of realizing that when she is not there it is because she is ill. The assumption makes her sad.

It does not matter what a person looks like – God loves us as we are. But do we Christians always do the same? Many churches now have slimming clubs. In some of these, members are weighed at every meeting and are told they are 'good' if they have lost weight and 'bad' if they have gained. It would be much more positive if such clubs were re-named 'healthy eating clubs' and less emphasis was placed on weight. As they stand at present, some do more harm than good and it is questionable whether they really should take place in the church, or whether they indicate that we are conforming to the world's standards.

In some congregations there are counsellors who are available to help people going through difficult situations. An announcement during the service or a note in a church magazine can draw attention to the fact that there are people who are very willing to talk with anyone who would like some support. In other churches there are groups such as 'share, prayer and care groups' where people can go for help.

Some people in the congregation might like to offer practical help to those with eating disorders. They might provide a lift to church or to a Bible study (as the sufferer will probably not own a car or use public transport, because she does not want to spend money on herself).

Christians sometimes tell a sufferer to let go of her problem and 'give it to God'. The sufferer can feel guilty because she cannot manage to do this. She is afraid of giving up her control, because that might mean that she would put on weight. The patient might be able to accept teaching which points out that we are weak but God is strong, and he can use even her if she will let him. She can be reminded that there is no need for her to do anything to earn God's love, because she is already precious in his sight. Bulimics and anorexics tend to feel that they must achieve in order to please others and to please God. When they are helped to get rid of this distorted view, they can begin truly to experience God's grace. The patient learns that God accepts her as she is, and is more pleased by her faith and her love for him than by sacrifices or works.

Patients in hospital are usually very grateful when people from the church visit them. The visitors who are most welcome are those who act in the way in which Jesus would act. Such visitors have a loving and not a judgmental or 'pushy' attitude. They are kind, caring and willing to chat or to listen, showing that the patient is worth their time and attention. Sometimes all that is wanted is someone who will be there, not necessarily saying anything. We might learn something even from the friends of Job. These men left their homes and their families, and wept and tore their clothes to show that they identified with Job. They did not say anything to him for the first week they sat with him. It was when they started to talk that they began to add to Job's burdens. Sometimes it is better to say nothing.

In some churches a visiting rota is set up so that not all the visitors descend on a patient at the same time. If the patient cannot attend church services she is likely to appreciate tapes of sermons. She may also be very glad when people offer to pray with her. Little gifts, such as a bunch of flowers, show her that you do care. As one bulimic said to me, 'It's harder to say that God can't love you when you are experiencing his love through his children. When they show you God's love, you realize he does care.'

There is a need for sensitivity when speaking with an anorexic or bulimic. It may seem natural to encourage her by saying, 'You are looking well', but this friendly greeting can terrify the sufferer who interprets it as implying, 'You are no longer underweight and in need of care', or even, 'Everyone can see that you have changed and are now looking fat.' Commenting on appearance also suggests that appearance is all-important. If you want to give praise, it is better to admire her for seeming more relaxed, showing her feelings, going out more, or taking part in more activities, rather than complimenting her for physical changes.

People in the church can help an anorexic or bulimic to identify her gifts, and encourage her to use them. She may feel untalented and worthless, but she should be shown that she has a part to play in the church. We are all part of the body of Christ, and each member is needed if the body is to function at its best. The sufferer might be invited to help with flower arranging, the Sunday school or a mother and toddler's group, or visiting people who are sick or elderly. Many bulimics and anorexics are talented at drama, writing or music. These skills can be used in the life of the church. Look for her good qualities. When people are given responsibility they become more confident. They also get to know others and feel more useful and accepting of themselves.

Members of a church may wish to offer support to the sufferer's family as well as to the patient herself. The mother of one anorexic said to me, 'It's not just my daughter who suffers from anorexia – the whole family suffers from it!'

When people from the church phone to ask the family how the patient is progressing, they show that they care. Consequently the parents of the patient feel less isolated. The family should not be blamed or criticized. The mother in particular is likely to be feeling very guilty and anxious. She will appreciate being given a chance to talk about what she is experiencing. It can be a nice gesture to give her flowers from the church, to show that she is being remembered. She may be very grateful for invitations to go out, as it does her good to get out of the house and start thinking about something other than her child's eating disorder. While I was in hospital my mother was invited to visit a craft fair in a rural hospital for people with mental and physical handicaps. As my mother does not drive, she was glad to get the chance of a drive in the country. When she saw the patients she realized that I could be considered healthy compared to many of them, and so started to feel a little less worried about my situation.

The parents of a child with an eating disorder may really appreciate it if they are invited out for an evening, or if their daughter is invited out. They can then relax and give attention to each other, instead of spending every moment worrying about the sufferer. They can be reminded that there is still a normal world outside the tense situation in which they have been living, and they may even be able to enjoy a meal together, for once not having to think about what food their daughter will accept.

In most churches a lot of social events take place. People spend time enjoying each others' company, and friendships are built up. Anorexics and bulimics often steer clear of such events if they think that food is likely to be involved – as it very often is. A sufferer's anxiety about social events might be reduced if she was told in advance what to expect in terms of food. For instance, it could be announced that 'there will be a self-service salad buffet', or 'sandwiches will be available for those who want them'. Alternatively, the sufferer might be asked to help serve, and told that she can help in the kitchen during the meal and eat something only if she wants to.

Anorexics and bulimics tend to be especially sensitive to issues regarding their sexual identity and their marital status, and so it is worth saying something about singleness. As nearly 40% of the people in the average church are single, the point applies not only to those with eating disorders.

A relatively high percentage of people with eating

disorders are unmarried. They tend to draw back from any intimate relationship, especially one with a member of the opposite sex. Some bulimics feel so worthless and lonely that they are willing to allow anyone to use their bodies; but in most cases women with eating disorders distrust men and find the thought of sex repulsive. At the same time they feel rejected because men do not show an interest in them (often because the women are too shy to encourage such interest). In the 'couple culture' in which we live, there is often a suggestion that a young man who has no female partner is 'queer', while a young woman who is unattached is pitied as it is assumed that she has been left 'on the shelf', unable to attract a man. A young person may want to remain single, but sense that others think him or her unusual for not having a close relationship with a person of the opposite sex.

Regrettably, this attitude is often present in the church as well as in society at large. Some churches would make good dating agencies! With the best of intentions, people will invite an unattached woman and a single man for lunch and leave them to 'get to know each other', much to the embarrassment of the two concerned. No wonder there is a divorce problem in the church – Christians are sometimes pressurized into a marriage they do not want, by well-meaning people who believe that one of the spiritual gifts is the gift of match-making. I can think of a friend who told me she had invited a young man to her house group because 'there is a lovely girl who goes and they would make such a nice couple'. The following week she asked me if I would go on a date with 'someone she knew' if she arranged it. When I declined, she invited me to her house group. Sure that she had ulterior motives, I invited her to join me for a Bible study instead!

Many churches are not very good at catering for

single people. 'Bring a partner' evenings and events for 'young marrieds' can leave unmarried people feeling lonely. At a wedding reception a single person is often asked, 'And when do you hope to get married?' This can be intended as an expression of hope for her future, or simply as a friendly conversation starter. While some single people are not at all bothered by such comments, the woman with an eating disorder is very sensitive to such remarks and interprets the question as a means of telling her, 'We cannot accept you as a single person.'

It is not uncommon for an event such as a church anniversary to be celebrated with a party which includes some form of dancing. A barn dance or a ceilidh usually offers an opportunity for everyone to join in, as partners are not really necessary for group dancing. Other types of dancing are meant for couples, so that someone who goes to the dance without a partner receives the message that she is incomplete, inadequate, a non-person.

Many single people either have no desire to dance or else have the confidence to ask someone on to the dance-floor. Some bulimics fall into this category. Not so the typical anorexic. She might go to a party in the hope that someone will ask her to dance, because even if she refuses she will have been in the powerful situation of being asked to do something, and her self-esteem will have been boosted. The offer of a dance, or even just a conversation, would mean far more to her than to the self-confident young women around her. But her dream may remain a dream. A tired, shy, pale, skeletal figure wearing no make-up or jewellery is easy to overlook. At celebrations people tend to seek out friends they know well and can joke with, not withdrawn, relative strangers who are hard to converse with because they say very little.

The anorexic may spend a whole party talking to old ladies, with a lump in her throat. She will wonder why

134

she is left out even at a Christian party. Because she has a pessimistic way of thinking, she is likely to conclude that she is the ugliest, most horrible, most untouchable thing in the world. I did, when I went to a Christian party and was left on my own. I sat watching a sword dance while the couples on the floor were having a break, and I longed to pick up the swords and cut myself into little pieces. I needed help. By becoming informed and by demonstrating care, churches can give the kind of help that is needed.

14
How can I find help?

My child, why are you hurting me?
I created you in my own image
So that I could have fellowship with you.
I looked forward to the time that we would spend
*   together.*
But you spend your time in a world of your own,
Worrying about your weight.

I made you a body, with bright eyes and rosy
*   cheeks,*
Arms to hug with, and a voice to laugh and sing.
But you say you hate my gift, your body, and you
*   want to destroy it.*
The twinkle has gone out of your eyes, and you are
*   silent.*
Your face is gaunt and pale, and cold hands hang
*   limply by your sides.*

Dear child, I gave you friends to share with,
But you hid away from them,
Never letting them know the real you; the you I
*   made.*
I send tasty foods for you to enjoy, and to bring you
*   health.*
You throw them back in my face.

I dwell in your heart.
Your body is a temple for the Holy Spirit.
But you have tried to pull down this temple
And ignore the Spirit within.
You say you are worthless,
Implying that my Spirit is worth nothing to you.

Loved one, I have great plans for you
For an exciting future in which you'll feel fulfilled.
But you are wasting your potential day by day.
I sent my Son to die so that you could live life to the
   full.
But you have chosen instead a living death.
I offer you forgiveness, but you refuse to accept it
And instead keep punishing yourself for mistakes of
   the past.

My child, I love you.
I long for you to spend time with me,
To stop worrying about how you look,
To think about me, not about food.
Won't you eat normally, just for me?
Won't you hand over your rituals, taking just one
   day at a time?
I never ask you to do anything impossible.
I know it's hard, I really do understand,
But I am strong, and I want to make you strong too.
   Trust me.
Please, won't you try? Because I love you, dear
   child.
I love you. Please listen to me now.

If you are at the moment a captive of an eating disorder, try to believe that freedom from this bondage is possible. Recovery usually takes a long time, but persevering is more than worth it. If you feel that you do not have the strength you need to make the changes which are necessary in your life, remind yourself that the Lord provides the strength to help us to overcome our problems. As we draw closer to him, the Healer, we find that we become more whole. A prayer that many people use is the serenity prayer: 'God, grant me the serenity to accept the things I cannot change, the courage to change the things I can, and the wisdom to know the difference.'

Next time you feel down, try to 'do unto others as you would have them do unto you'. For example, you might visit somebody who lives alone, write a letter to cheer someone up, or make or buy a token gift for a friend. Such acts of kindness help you to forget your own worries, and will make you feel happier as you see the appreciation of the recipient. You will think better of yourself for caring. As Karl Menninger, a psychiatrist, has said, 'Love cures two people: the one who receives it, and the one who gives it.'

You are likely to have some set-backs in your journey into wholeness, but these need not be seen as failures or as proof that you will never make it. How you view a slip is the main determinant of whether it will be a temporary lapse or the start of a relapse. After a bad day you can practise saying to yourself, 'I've been doing really well. Today my old ways tried to reappear, but that doesn't mean I'm back to square one. I do want to continue getting better, so I'm going to eat properly right now. By doing that I'll show great strength and determination. Today is a battle won, not lost.'

You should seek to cast out destructive thoughts, countering them with positive truths. Saying something aloud over and over again helps you to believe it. The words you have been rehearsing may automatically spring to mind when negative thoughts threaten to emerge. Some examples of the kinds of negative statements people with eating disorders often make are given below, along with the truths which should replace them:

'I'm ugly and horrible' can be replaced with 'I have been made in God's image, and he lives in me';

'I'm unlovable' with 'God loves me exactly as I am, and is working in my life';

'I can never get better' with 'God is making me whole';

'I can't do this' with 'I can do all things *through Christ* who strengthens me.'

More examples of negative thoughts and the truths which counteract them are available from Anorexia and Bulimia Care (ABC). (Send four second-class stamps and ask for *The Truth Can Set You Free*.) Try also to use your own words to affirm your worth, so that your destructive thought patterns can be reprogrammed.

If you would like to correspond with someone you can relate to, someone who has had an eating disorder and has recovered, write to ABC. People who have recovered from eating disorders are living proof that it is possible to overcome an eating disorder and replace a living death with 'life in all its fullness' (John 10:10, GNB).

As human beings we tend to make a mess of things. Ever since Eve and Adam rebelled against God in the Garden of Eden, men and women have been marring God's perfect world. But God can take the worst situation and bring something wonderful out of it. He allowed Jesus to be crucified and the world to go dark, and then he raised Christ from the dead. If we offer him

140

our lives he can take these too, and turn the mess that we are in into a beautiful offering to him. Like the butterfly which emerges from the destructive caterpillar, we can become a new creation, something completely different.

I have seen something of this in El Salvador, a country where I recently spent one month. In 1992 a Peace Agreement was signed in that country to end twelve years of civil war. Terrible atrocities had taken place during the war. On my first afternoon in El Salvador I stood at the top of a hill looking down on the land, and admired the breath-taking view. Then I discovered that during the war the Death Squads took men up this hill, tied their thumbs behind their backs with barbed wire, and made them walk over the edge to their graves. The only crime of those murdered was that they spoke up for the oppressed. The place is known as 'Devil's Gate'. Man has made a haven of beauty into a place of murder.

The next day, in contrast, I met a man who had turned a place of murder into a haven of beauty. On 16 November 1989 six Jesuit priests were murdered at a Catholic university, along with their housekeeper and her daughter. I went to visit the place where they had been killed, and I met the man whose wife and daughter were among the dead. This man is the gardener at the university, and he has planted a circle of eight red rosebushes (with two yellow bushes in the centre) in the spot where the eight corpses once lay. He spoke to me about his faith in God, with no trace of bitterness about what had happened. He has made something beautiful out of something horrific. God can make something beautiful out of our lives, if we allow him to. God is always there waiting to bring the light of day even into the darkest of nights. There is always hope.

Appendix A
Professional help

General Practitioner (G.P.)

The G.P. is often the first person contacted by someone suffering from an eating disorder. As doctors are trained to treat a huge variety of conditions, it is hardly surprising that not every doctor is a specialist in eating disorders. Nevertheless, the G.P. can be a valuable source of help. Unfortunately not every G.P. is helpful. Occasionally a doctor fails to pick up what the problem really is, especially if the anorexic or bulimic is not open about her eating habits and her fear of gaining weight. People with eating disorders are very good at disguising weight loss and denying that there is a problem. G.P.s have been known to dismiss lightly a mother who reports the patient's loss of weight, classifying her as an 'over-anxious parent' who should stop fussing. If the doctor joins the patient in denying that there is anything wrong, the mother is at a loss to know what to do next. This is very unfortunate, because the earlier an eating disorder is treated the more favourable the outcome is likely to be.

Sometimes a bulimic who has plucked up the courage to ask for help feels unable to admit the extent of her bingeing and purging, and is dismissed by a doctor who tells her that she looks fine and should stop worrying about her weight. An anorexic who pretends that she is not deliberately losing weight can be simply told to eat more fattening foods, without the doctor realizing that she would be terrified to do so. Try to persevere and find another professional who does understand, instead of giving up.

143

Often patients go to the doctor about a specific symptom, such as difficulties sleeping or concentrating, or missing monthly periods. The doctor may be able to point out that the symptom is caused by an inadequate diet or by the use of vomiting or laxatives, and can give the patient advice about a more healthy approach to food. The G.P. can also carry out tests, for example to see if the patient is anaemic.

However, the G.P. only has a limited amount of time to spend with each patient – often just five minutes – and may wish to refer the patient to a specialist who can offer her more time and more specialized advice.

Some G.P.s routinely send anorexics and bulimics for medical tests, such as blood tests or pelvic ultra scans. Not only do these provide the doctor with a picture of any physical symptoms which should receive attention, but the results may also bring home to the patient herself just how much harm she is doing her body. Many patients find it hard to believe how much damage they are doing to themselves until they see the results of these tests. Although they might have been told facts about the consequences of eating disorders, they rarely apply these facts to themselves. A nurse who has anorexia may know in theory what a healthy diet is and how many calories are needed each day, yet still believe that she can live on a quarter of this requirement. She might study books recording the effects of malnutrition but feel that what she is reading does not apply to her. If she is shown a scan revealing her own bone loss, this can help her to realize that she really could fracture a major bone or even end up in a wheelchair if she continues her restrictive diet. When this strikes home she may become willing to receive help, and more determined to change. Support should be available in addition to information.

Dietitian

The G.P. might refer the patient on to a dietitian. A dietitian has knowledge about nutrition and the components of a healthy diet. He or she is able to explain what happens to food after it has been eaten. This can be reassuring to patients who think that unless they force the food out it must remain in their bodies and turn into fat. The dietitian can explain why different nutrients are necessary, and discuss any symptoms which may have been caused by an inadequate diet.

The dietitian can also explain the consequences of bingeing and vomiting and of laxative abuse. He or she can point out, for example, that the metabolic rate is lowered by a pattern of starving and bingeing, which means that the body requires less energy (and fewer calories) to run on. The dietitian can also explain why there may be some fluid retention for a short time after bingeing and purging stop. If the patient is exercising a lot, she can be reminded that muscle is heavier than fat, and if she is not losing weight this does not mean that she is getting fat.

The dietitian may help the anorexic or bulimic to plan out a balanced diet which she is willing to try. Together they can discuss what a 'normal meal' might consist of. If the anorexic or bulimic feels safe only when she eats exactly the same thing every day, the dietitian can use this as a starting point, perhaps helping the patient to add to her choices little by little, and making sure that the chosen meals include all the essential nutrients. The dietitian can draw attention to the good in food (such as the calcium which is necessary for strong bones), and may even refer to food as a 'medicine', to help the patient feel less guilty about eating.

The anorexic who panics when she sees 'a mountain of food' and feels unable to tackle large meals might be encouraged to eat 'little and often'. For instance, she might eat six meals during the day, each containing 400–600 calories. She is likely to feel less guilty and less out of control eating small portions than she would with larger meals, and she is also less likely to feel bloated afterwards.

The dietitian might encourage a bulimic to eat healthy snacks throughout the day, rather than starving all day which produces a craving for a binge in the evening. If the bulimic craves for a particular substance (such as chocolate) when she binges, she should be encouraged to build this 'binge food' into her normal diet, allowing herself to eat a little of it from time to time without feeling guilty. In this way the feeling of deprivation and craving which causes the binge does not arise, as she realizes that there is no forbidden food. The bulimic might be encouraged to eat more hot food, as heat increases the feeling of satiety or fullness and can reduce the desire to binge. The anorexic, on the other hand, may be encouraged to eat cold foods, so that she does not feel bloated.

The dietitian may encourage the patient to record everything she eats in a food diary, so that they can discuss together how adequate her diet is, and any changes she might make. Some dietitians weigh their patients and calculate how much they need to eat in order to maintain or to increase their weight.

Christian carers

Religion is very important to many individuals with eating disorders, and some patients look for a Christian counsellor because secular therapists may tend to ignore the spiritual side of life, the 'God-shaped hole in our lives'. A Christian counsellor relies on God for guidance and would like to see the patient becoming dependent on God rather than on anyone or anything else. Most Christians are prepared to see a sufferer whether or not she is a Christian. They do not try to force the patient to accept their beliefs, although they are very willing to discuss these beliefs if she requests this. They treat the patient with love and respect, knowing that she has been created by God and in his image. They may offer to pray with the patient, if she would like this. In this way the anorexic or bulimic can receive strength from God, for whom nothing is impossible. She may also begin to see her problems in perspective, and gain a reason for living.

Anorexia and Bulimia Care helps to link sufferers with Christian 'carers', who do not necessarily have professional training but often have either recovered from an eating disorder themselves or have cared for a friend or family member who has been a sufferer. If the carer lives near the sufferer they may meet up. Otherwise they communicate through letters, and perhaps phone-calls. Many sufferers prefer to write to rather than meet their carer, perhaps because they feel so unhappy about their bodies that they prefer not to be seen. Letters can be less threatening than face-to-face encounters. Probing questions can be ignored more easily if they come in a letter than if they are spoken. When concentration is poor, it can be easier to write a letter (which can be written a little at a time) than to follow a conversation. A letter which comes in reply can be kept and referred to again, in a way that a normal conversation cannot. Some sufferers are shy or anxious in social situations and have difficulty in 'finding the right words'. They prefer to write letters as they do not have to think of what to say on the spot when communicating by post. Often sufferers find it therapeutic to write down all their thoughts in a letter, because seeing their thoughts in writing helps them to clarify in their own minds what the issues are.

Counsellors

In Britain anyone can call themselves a counsellor or a psychotherapist, so one should be careful when seeking counselling outside the National Health Service. A potential client has every right to ask about the qualifications of the therapist. In fact, the client should ask all the questions she has on her mind before making the decision to see a particular therapist. A therapist should want what is best for the individual client, and should be willing to suggest that the client try an alternative if she is looking for something which they do not offer. If the therapist appears to be interested only in recruiting patients (and their fees), that therapist should be turned down. There is no point in going to see someone who is only concerned with making a profit. That is not the kind of person a client wants to spend a lot of time with. The client needs to find a therapist with whom she feels comfortable.

It is advisable to look for a therapist who has experience of working with patients with eating disorders. Otherwise he or she may make unrealistic suggestions.

The relationship which the client has with the therapist is very important. When therapists are only temporary, or frequently away at conferences or on holiday, this can prevent the patient from being willing to open up and develop a relationship of trust. It is better if the therapist is available for a longer period. The therapist should offer understanding and warmth, and value the client as a person, thus building up her self-esteem. As control is of fundamental importance to the patient, it has often been suggested that the therapist should not take too much control. Rather than telling the client what she should be feeling and thinking, and imposing one's own interpretations on her experiences, a good counsellor will encourage her to express what

148

she experiences, and support her in making her own decisions.

The Citizens Advice Bureau and the Samaritans usually have information about self-help groups and counselling services available in the area. The British Association for Counselling also has information. There may also be local addresses in the Yellow Pages. The Eating Disorders Association produces a register of professionals available to help people with eating disorders, divided into geographical areas.

Psychiatrist or psychologist

Some health centres, G.P.s and places of work have their own counsellors or psychologists, but most do not. To receive this help on the National Health Service, a referral from a G.P. is necessary. NHS help has the advantage of being free or at a low cost, but has the drawback of a long waiting list.

Many G.P.s do refer anorexics and bulimics on to clinical psychologists or to psychiatrists. It is unfortunate that in Britain there is still a stigma associated with seeking psychological help, as such a visit can be very effective. In the United States the pendulum has swung the other way, and it is almost a status symbol to have seen one's therapist.

I am often asked, 'What is the difference between a psychiatrist and a psychologist?' The answer to this might be, 'Several thousand pounds a year.' Psychiatrists and psychologists often do similar work, but the training is different, and so are the wages!

Clinical psychologists are people who have obtained a degree in psychology and then received at least two further years of clinical training, usually after a period of relevant work or research experience.

Psychiatrists are people who have qualified as medical

doctors, and then have specialized in psychiatry. Often a large part of the psychiatric training involves learning about biochemical imbalances in the body which may play a part in certain psychiatric conditions, and training the psychiatrist to administer drugs to the mentally ill.

The types of treatments offered by counsellors, psychotherapists, psychologists and psychiatrists are outlined in Appendix B.

Appendix B
Types of treatment

A wide variety of treatments have been used with patients suffering from anorexia and bulimia, ranging from art, dance, music or poetry therapy, through aromatherapy, hypnotherapy and acupuncture, to electroconvulsive therapy and surgery such as leucotomy. Some therapies involve animals – many sufferers have a great love for animals and claim that animals, unlike humans, give them unconditional love. Some patients take part in horse-riding therapy (which is said to raise self-esteem, as you must sit high when riding), and even swimming with dolphins has been recommended!

It would seem that proponents of almost every conceivable treatment can boast some successes, while no one treatment 'works' for every patient. Different patients prefer different approaches. Some of the approaches most commonly used in the treatment of anorexics and bulimics are discussed below.

Counselling and psychotherapy

Counselling tends to be used for a specific problem such as coping with bereavement, a particular phobia, or an eating disorder. A problem-solving approach is taken. The counsellor may give practical advice on overcoming the problem, focusing on the present rather than the past.

A psychologist is more likely to focus on general dissatisfaction or unhappiness with life rather than the particular condition, and to look beneath the surface for root causes. The psychologist or psychiatrist will probably begin by having a long talk with the patient about how the eating disorder began, and the types of things which might have played a causal role. The patient will also have an opportunity to discuss whatever is currently upsetting her. This type of psychotherapy tends to be more long-term than counselling, often continuing for months or years.

The anorexic or bulimic may benefit from either short-term counselling or long-term psychotherapy. Both try to help the patient to reach a greater self-awareness.

Behaviour therapy

One criticism of some types of psychotherapy is that they can involve discussion alone. Although the client may develop insight into her condition, she will not necessarily change her behaviour. In order to avoid this problem, some therapists 'reward' or 'punish' the patient depending on her behaviour. The reward or punishment does not need to be tangible – it might merely be showing pleasure when the client behaves in a healthy manner and displeasure or disappointment when she does not. In other instances the therapist asks the patient to buy herself a treat when she takes a step forward, providing her own reward.

The focus is very much on the patient's behaviour, and she might be asked to write in a diary everything she eats, and her feelings at the time. Having to monitor what she is eating can help her to improve her eating habits, as she now feels accountable. She is praised for accurate monitoring, and for all signs of progress. The diary can be used to help identify triggers. Measures which might help her to change her behaviour are recommended (for example, alternative ways to deal with anger; and shopping when she is not hungry, using a list so that she does not buy in 'binge' foods).

She may also receive training in relaxation techniques, and in improving her social skills and becoming more assertive.

Cognitive therapy

Those who offer cognitive therapy believe that it is important not only that the disordered eating is corrected, but also that the anorexic or bulimic comes to accept herself, and is made aware of her faulty patterns of thinking (cognitions) and how she can respond to them.

Anorexics and bulimics have irrational patterns of thought. Some of these are similar to the thought processes of depressed people, who automatically take a pessimistic view of events and interpret happenings in such a way that they blame themselves. For instance, if a friend stops writing to them they conclude that this must be because their letters are boring, when in fact the real reason has nothing to do with this.

The anorexic or bulimic tends to over-generalize (for example, saying, 'When I used to eat carbohydrates I was fat, so if I eat any again I will become fat once more'), and to enagage in what is known as personalization, taking everything personally (for instance assuming that if people laugh when she passes them in the street they must be laughing at her). She is also likely to draw conclusions from insufficient evidence, while ignoring contradictory evidence (an anorexic might say, 'I can't control myself – I ate everything that I was served at lunchtime'). People with eating disorders may also overestimate the undesirable consequences of events (thinking, 'If I don't pass this exam I'll never get a job' or 'If I gain another ounce I'll look like a beached whale').

During the course of cognitive therapy, the therapist

helps the patient to identify such distorted thoughts and to change them. The therapist might draw attention to these beliefs by saying something like, 'You say that people will like you only if you do not gain any weight. Do *you* only choose friends who are thin? Have you noticed whether my weight has changed since last week?' The patient may then realize that she judges herself by standards which she would not apply to other people, and she may come to the stage where she can accept a gain in her weight, and realize that weight does not need to be the most important factor in her life.

If the patient sets very high standards for herself (as most people with eating disorders do), the therapist may challenge this. The patient might be persuaded to stop doing only what she believes she 'should' do, and to start doing things which she herself would like to do.

Cognitive and behavioural approaches to therapy are often combined, forming cognitive-behavioural therapy. This has achieved a fair degree of success in modifying the attitudes of people with eating disorders, and bringing about long-term changes in behaviour. However, the patient must be motivated and prepared to work hard for the therapy to reach its full potential to help. The desire to change is all-important, as hinted at in the joke:

'How many psychologists does it take to change a lightbulb?'
'Five. One to hold the bulb, and four to hold a case conference as to whether the bulb really wants to change.'

Drug treatment

Drug treatment alone is generally of little long-term benefit to anorexics and bulimics, but medication can be

154

beneficial, especially for bulimia, when used along with psychotherapy. Any physiological abnormalities are likely to be a direct result of malnutrition, induced vomiting and laxative abuse. They usually disappear as these are corrected, without needing any medication to put them right.

Having said that, there is little doubt that some of the symptoms of anorexia and bulimia can be eased by some drugs. For instance, undernutrition causes sleeping problems, and mild sleeping pills can be effective in reducing this symptom. After sleeping disturbances have been treated, the patient has more energy available to devote to overcoming her problems. There are also drugs which have been found to have some success in reducing the number of episodes of binge-eating or the size of the binges.

Antidepressants have also been widely used, helping to combat the depressive symptoms which commonly accompany anorexia and bulimia. Patients with eating disorders may be better able to cope with stressful situations when maintained on antidepressants.

Antidepressant medication may be of most benefit when a sufferer really does want to conquer her eating disorder, but feels so low that she cannot summon up the effort to make the necessary changes in her life. After taking the drugs, she may feel better able to make positive changes. Treating her negative mood may help her to break the habit of bingeing, as binges are most likely to occur when the patient feels unhappy. The patient should also receive assistance in developing alternative methods of dealing with depressive feelings, so that she will not act impulsively when she experiences such feelings in the future.

During the course of anorexia or bulimia the sufferer is likely to isolate herself from other people. A prescription of minor tranquillizers can sometimes help her to

155

overcome her anxiety about social encounters, and take a step towards building up a supportive social network. The patient should not be made to feel guilty for taking prescribed medication for a time, any more than a diabetic should be criticized for taking insulin.

Minor tranquillizers have very few side-effects, and generally make the patient feel pleasant and more satisfied with life. When calmed and free from anxiety, the patient feels more in control of her life. Some drugs do have side-effects for a number of patients, for example causing constipation, or an appetite increase, or a weight gain. The patient can always ask the person prescribing them if there are likely to be any side-effects. It is important that she tells the doctor about the eating pattern and not just the anxiety or depression, because some drugs (such as chlorpromazine and lithium) should not be given to people who severely restrict their food intake, induce vomiting or abuse laxatives.

Patients can feel misunderstood and conclude that they are not worth bothering about if a physician dismisses them with a bottle of pills instead of taking time to listen to them. Many anorexics and bulimics think of drugs as 'bad' substances which make them feel out of control, helpless and inadequate. Some refuse to take their medication, or else swallow it but then 'vomit it out'. The patient should look for a professional to talk to, whether or not medication is prescribed – drugs alone are not enough. No drug can raise a patient's self-respect or cause her to stop overvaluing thinness. When drug treatment alone is used and a patient is not helped to deal with factors which underlie her eating disorder and to develop more adaptive coping strategies, she is likely to relapse in times of stress. Anorexia and bulimia involve more than disorderly eating. When medication is stopped, the problems are still likely to be present, and so it is important that the patient finds someone who will provide supportive help and advice, enabling her to make behavioural changes and maintain these after the medication has been stopped.

In-patient treatment

Sometimes an anorexic who is severely malnourished, or a woman who is causing a lot of damage to her body by bingeing and vomiting, is advised to go into hospital. If she refuses, it is possible that she will be admitted to hospital against her will ('sectioned'), as a life-saving measure.

Anorexics usually remain in hospital for a number of months. Gaining weight is a slow process, as 3,500 extra calories are needed for every pound of weight gain. Although the patient might appear to gain weight rapidly at first, most of this gain will be due to water as she has been dehydrated, and the rapid weight gain will not continue. The stomach shrinks when very little food is eaten and so she will probably feel uncomfortable and bloated when she first starts to eat more. With time her stomach will readjust to food and her metabolic rate will rise. After feeling worse for a short time, she will then begin to feel much better and realize that it is worth it. But she may need reassurance during those first few days.

In most re-feeding programmes the number of calories given is increased gradually. If the patient completely refuses food, she is likely to be fed through a tube. Otherwise she will probably receive normal meals (so that she becomes accustomed to them) and high-calorie drinks to provide the extra energy which is required. Usually she is prevented from eating too much as well as too little, as it would be undesirable if she began to binge-eat in order to be discharged sooner.

While I was in hospital myself, I sometimes wished

that there was a drug, with no undesirable side-effects, which when taken just once would make me a normal (or preferably just below average) weight. I thought that becoming a normal weight would bring with it a great sense of relief, although this would only last as long as there was no chance that I would go on to become overweight. Eating in order to gain weight seemed too self-indulgent, and too out of control. It also took a very long time. In reality, I would almost certainly have found a dramatic weight gain very frightening, as it takes time to adjust to one's changing shape. Often anorexics who are treated as in-patients remain in the hospital for a 'maintenance period' after they have reached their target weight. This allows them to get used to their new weight, and to learn how much they will need to eat in order to maintain that weight. When they discover that their weight is not going to continue rising, but can remain stable, some of the panic (which might have led them to diet immediately had they been discharged at this stage) is removed.

Bulimics are treated as in-patients less often than anorexics, partly because there is a general lack of hospital beds and so the only patients with eating disorders admitted are cases where starvation has become life-threatening. Bulimics who do receive in-patient treatment usually do so at their own request. They are generally determined to break the binge-purge cycle, but believe that they will never succeed on their own. They wish to surrender themselves to constant supervision for a period, so that they will be unable to binge and purge and they will break the habit. In addition to supervision they receive support. As they are highly motivated, they often do well.

Hospitals vary considerably in the treatment offered. Some young anorexics and bulimics are treated in adolescent units, alongside adolescents who have been admitted because of drug or alcohol abuse, violent episodes and other forms of anti-social behaviour. Being with adolescents from different backgrounds can be interesting and is sometimes beneficial, but a timid anorexic can feel very distressed and threatened when confined with angry, uncontrollable adolescents, who may victimize her.

Another possibility is that she will be treated in a general psychiatric or medical ward. Here the nursing staff may be intolerant of a patient who has an eating disorder, feeling that her ill-health is her own fault. As hospital beds are scarce and many hospitals are short of staff, some nurses resent it when a patient with anorexia or bulimia takes up all their time, especially if she must be observed continually. A number of nurses also feel some hidden jealousy because they would like to lose weight themselves.

The patient may be met with more understanding if she is treated in a ward which specializes in eating disorders. Staff who are trained in working with people with eating disorders are less likely to be hostile towards these patients, or to be manipulated or deceived by them. They tend to react with more sensitivity, tact and patience towards this particular group of patients – although, of course, this is not always the case, and some staff who are not specialized in this area also show all these qualities. When patients with eating disorders are treated together they realize that there are other people like them, and they feel less isolated and different. However, there may be problems as anorexics are always likely to compare themselves with each other and want to be the thinnest; and bulimics may 'gang up' against the staff, teaching each other 'tricks'.

In some special units the importance of exercise to the anorexic is acknowledged, and she is given physiotherapy and allowed to go for walks and even spend time in a gymnasium as long as she also eats a sufficient amount. Even in a friendly environment there is rarely if ever a need to worry that the patient might enjoy the attention so much that she will not be motivated to make the progress necessary to get out and stay out.

Some hospitals use 'behavioural' techniques, giving patients privileges as a 'reward' for keeping meals down or for gaining weight. In extreme cases patients are locked in a room and not allowed to receive visitors or phone-calls, or even to read books or watch television, until they have gained weight. This is not the most helpful approach. Unless patients are helped to change their attitudes, they are likely to return to old habits after they have been 'released'. A high proportion relapse very soon after being discharged and are suspicious of any subsequent therapy. Others progress from anorexia to bulimia, or become compulsive eaters. This course of events is related to the fact that while in hospital they learned to consume everything placed in front of them and were not helped to perceive their body signals or to establish a normal eating pattern.

Not surprisingly, some therapists urge that one should only hospitalize anorexics and bulimics if they desire it or else as a last resort. On a more positive note, although anorexics may resent in-patient treatment at the time, retrospectively many say that it was helpful. Even among those admitted against their will, more than half later agree that hospitalization was helpful.

When a patient is severely emaciated, to the extent of being less than 75% of her ideal weight, she is unlikely to be able to concentrate on or make use of psychotherapy, and so such therapy is not offered. The first priority in this instance is to increase her weight. Most anorexics and bulimics above this weight do receive some form of psychotherapy while they are in hospital.

Before agreeing to go into hospital the patient can

160

always ask what the treatment will be like, and what sort of ward it will be. She may even be given a tour of the ward. She has the right to say what treatment she thinks will be best for her.

Hypnotherapy

Few Christians have spoken favourably of hypnosis. Christians tend to warn against putting the mind into a passive state, and opening oneself to the influence of a hypnotist. The Bible never encourages us to empty our minds, stating instead that we should fill our minds with the things of God (Philippians 4:8).

Even many secular psychologists doubt the effectiveness of hypnotherapy, believing any beneficial outcome to be more a result of a good relationship with a therapist than of the hypnosis itself. There is little evidence that hypnosis itself 'works', in the sense of producing an altered state of mind. The results of hypnosis often can be explained in terms of beliefs, expectations and conformity. What the patient believes in may 'work' for her, or else she might merely conform to what the hypnotist says, just as she conforms to what a doctor recommends.

Some patients benefit simply from having a hypnotist help them to relax and then giving sensible advice. For instance, in the case of a patient with an eating disorder the hypnotist might say, 'You can sample fattening foods occasionally and not panic . . . you will follow a sensible, nourishing diet . . .' A patient does not have to be hypnotized to be helped by such advice.

Some hypnotherapists do use more sophisticated techniques. They help clients to think about their past and to recall events and traumas which they appear to have forgotten. Often these could have been recalled had anyone helped the client to relax, to remember the context of the event, and to concentrate for a considerable time on bringing the event to memory. The hypnotist does all of this as well as claiming to put the patient in a 'trance'. Sometimes what the client 'remembers' under hypnosis is later discredited as it can be proven to have never happened. In such instances the patient was trying so hard to produce a 'memory' that she actually made something up and thought it must be true.

As control is very important to people with eating disorders, they often feel unwilling to surrender themselves to a hypnotist. Some patients even feel vulnerable when they sleep naturally. They are terrified when asked to drop their guard in front of a hypnotherapist and to conform to his suggestions. After all, he might succeed in persuading her to eat, which is what she is most afraid of. Individuals with anorexia nervosa may therefore be 'unhypnotizable', unwilling to drop their defences and be open to suggestions. In addition, they find it difficult to relax and are too preoccupied with thoughts about food and weight to concentrate on what the hypnotist is saying. Bulimics, on the other hand, have been found to be generally hypnotizable. This may be because they are used to entering a trance-like 'dissociated state', because during binges they feel dissociated from their real selves.

If a patient wants to receive hypnotherapy and makes a commitment to this treatment process, she may find it helpful. She should not be made to feel guilty for choosing this form of treatment. If she believes in hypnosis and the hypnotist is a good therapist with high ethical standards, there is no reason why she should not find the sessions very beneficial (although not necessarily any more so than any other treatment which she believes in). If, under hypnosis, suggestions are made associating eating with pleasant memories, she may start to feel more happy and relaxed when she eats.

When memories have been suppressed this tends to be because they have been too painful to face. If such memories rise to the surface during any form of treatment, the patient should be helped to work through the problems. She should receive support in doing so in the weeks which follow, and not just in one therapy session.

Group therapy and support groups

Some clients prefer to join therapy groups instead of (or as well as) engaging in individual therapy. Groups can be especially beneficial for people who find one-to-one sessions intimidating or threatening, and those who would become too dependent on the therapist if they received individual treatment. On a purely practical level, where payment is necessary group therapy tends to be much less expensive than individual counselling. On the other hand, groups are not suited to all patients. Those who are likely to compete with others in a group, wanting to be the thinnest or the most ill, are less likely to be helped by group treatment.

It does take a lot of courage to go to a group. Some patients will even go all the way to the meeting place, perhaps by train or taxi, and then will panic at the thought of admitting to a whole roomful of people that they have an eating disorder, and go back home.

There is a difference between formal group therapy and self-help or support groups. Group therapy is run by a professional, who sets the agenda and makes the decision about who may join the group. The group members are usually asked not to contact each other outside the group sessions. Self-help or support groups, on the other hand, tend to be organized by people who have had eating disorders rather than by professionals.

While the aim of group therapy is to get rid of anorexic or bulimic habits, self-help groups place less emphasis on 'curing' the patient, and more on offering her support. Participants are encouraged to contact and support one other outside the meetings. There may be a library of relevant books and tapes which group members can borrow.

Therapy groups usually consist of between six and twelve people. Some groups are 'open', meaning that newcomers can join the group and members can leave. Other groups are 'closed', with the same people present at each meeting. In closed groups there is a special sense of commitment, trust and continuity as there is no need to explain to newcomers what has been happening in the group in previous weeks.

The members of the group may all suffer from the same eating disorder or may have different symptoms. Some support groups are open to people caring for someone who has an eating disorder as well as to the sufferers themselves.

Within a group there is the opportunity to develop social skills, build up friendships, and discover that other people have had similar experiences. Members can identify with one another. They may be willing to share their secrets when they discover that others are in a similar situation and so understand what they mean. Feelings of loneliness and isolation are reduced by this process. However, it can take quite a long time for people with eating disorders to build up enough trust to begin to share their true feelings.

When one group member talks about a particular problem, others who have experienced similar difficulties can suggest ways in which it might be approached. Members can also learn new ways of behaving simply by observing others in the group. For example, an anorexic might notice that another member of the group shows her emotions, and realize that it can be a good thing to allow feelings to surface. Peers can point out and challenge the irrational thought patterns of a member of the group – although this should be done with great sensitivity, so that the sufferer does not feel destroyed by criticism.

If group decisions are made, group members have a chance to learn to negotiate – although it may be difficult to persuade some members to say what they really feel, instead of merely going along with everyone else. Group members may make a contract with each other, perhaps promising to try to stop bingeing or to stop losing weight. They are then accountable to each other. Participants can help and support one another. Through realizing that they have something to contribute, self-esteem is raised.

Those who are making their first steps towards recovery can be encouraged when they see how far others have come. They are in contact with people who are now happy and free from their eating disorder, and are helping to lead the group. A group member who is doing well may be given a leadership role. This will raise her self-esteem as she discovers how much help she can be to newer members of the group. It might also increase her determination not to slip back into her old ways, as she is now considered (by herself and by others) to be recovered.

In some groups use is made of techniques such as psychodrama. Here a sufferer may act out an experience from her past, with help from others in the group. Through this experience she may be able to bring to the surface memories which she has suppressed. She may also get in touch with feelings which she has bottled up.

Role-play may be used as a form of teaching, to provide group members with training in social skills by letting them practise what they might say and do in different situations. After one member has acted out a situation (such as a family discussion), others make comments about how she could react differently. They might suggest that she acts out the scene again but this time tries to negotiate instead of letting her own wishes be crushed, and tells people how she is really feeling instead of pretending that everything is fine. With practice, she will become more confident.

Some groups have sessions of assertiveness training. Many anorexics and bulimics believe that they should never be assertive because this would mean that they were selfish, arrogant or aggressive. But in actual fact assertiveness involves expressing one's true feelings instead of bottling them up, and can be a very positive quality. Anorexics and bulimics tend to be eager to please others and to avoid conflict. They do what others want them to do instead of what they themselves want. During assertiveness training they practise making their own wishes known, for instance saying, 'I can't help you this evening as I have made other plans.' When they put this into practice, they discover that people do not usually dislike them for being honest. They themselves feel more worthwhile and less pushed about because they have begun to look after themselves.

In some therapy groups patients are taught various relaxation techniques and different ways of coping with anxiety. Other groups make use of methods such as poetry therapy. It is common for an anorexic or bulimic to express in her diary or in poems feelings which she is unable to talk about openly. Poetry therapy involves reading and then creating poems, and discussing the feelings articulated within them. Writing or interpreting poetry from a novel viewpoint can help one to see things from a new perspective. The sufferer's feeling of powerlessness can be reduced when she creates characters in a poem or story over whom she has total control.

Moreover, when her own poetry is admired by others she feels understood, and more self-confident.

In some groups art or dance therapy is used for similar reasons. The members of the group express in movement or in drawings feelings which they may be unable to speak about. Verbal defences are bypassed, and the symbolic content of these non-verbal mediums can be explored. These techniques can also be used in individual therapy, and are especially useful when working with young children with eating disorders.

Family therapy

The influence of family relationships on the development of anorexia nervosa has been discussed since the earliest reports of the condition. Family therapists believe that the problem does not belong solely to the child; the whole family is responsible for the abnormal eating patterns. It is certainly true that a child's upbringing will influence her attitudes and her values.

If a patient is still living with her family, family therapy can be very useful, helping the whole family to understand each other more and to change for the better. Both the patient and the rest of the family tend to find family therapy stressful. Even so, finding something distressing is not necessarily a reason to avoid it. Most types of therapy involve talking about difficult issues, but taking the risk to do this can open the way to changes for the better.

The family may find it difficult to know how to react to the changes which they notice in their child as she proceeds with treatment. This is especially the case if she has been away from them in hospital. When she returns home she will have changed. The rest of the family may also need to change to accommodate this and to support her. Otherwise, she may fail to put into practice what she has learned during therapy.

The family should be warned that the patient may start to argue and to cry more frequently. They should not think that she is getting worse or suffering from a 'breakdown' if they notice such changes. A therapist can also explain that when the patient starts to stand up for herself and to become more independent, instead of complying to the wishes of everyone around her, this is a step forward. It need not be seen as an upsetting rebellion.

If the family are not involved in therapy they may feel excluded and scared of doing something wrong. In fact, there is often no right or wrong way to act, as long as they show their child love. For a long time after she is discharged they are likely to be afraid that she will relapse. They may watch her closely and be very careful about what they say. This creates a somewhat unnatural atmosphere in the home, and a certain degree of tension. In some homes, in contrast, everyone pretends that nothing has happened, or at least that it is all in the past. This is because they have not been able to come to terms with the fact that a member of the family has had an eating disorder.

Ideally, family therapy should involve the whole family, or at least everyone who still lives at home. If only the mother has any real contact with the patient, then the therapist might suggest how the father and siblings can support the mother. The parents should be encouraged to avoid giving the patient conflicting messages – the mother and father should try to work together. This does not mean that they must pretend to agree on every issue. It is helpful if the patient can see that it is possible to negotiate and come to an agreement.

Often the family feels ashamed about receiving treatment. It should be borne in mind that seeking help, whether as an individual or as a family, is a demonstration of strength and not of weakness. The aim of therapy is certainly not to attach blame to anyone. It is never helpful to say that the mother, or any other scapegoat, is to 'blame' for the anorexia. Explaining that anyone can be drawn into anorexia or bulimia without being aware of it can help reduce the guilt which is felt both by the patient and her family.

The therapist should explain clearly the rationale for therapy. The family might be asked what they would like to get out of the treatment process. One aim might be to help each member of the family to become more open about problems. The family might be encouraged to work at creating an honest atmosphere, where feelings can be shared. In this way difficulties can be faced with the help of the family instead of bottled up behind a façade of coping. The family might use the therapy time to examine unhealthy patterns and behaviours which have developed in the home, such as blaming each other, over-protectiveness and preventing independence, avoiding problems, or pretending instead of being honest.

Some family therapists use psychological techniques to aid discussion. For instance, members of the family might be asked to make a 'family sculpt', creating a picture of the family as they see it. This might be done as a drawing or a model. The family members can then discuss the sculpts, talking about which members of the family are close to each other in the drawing, and who is on their own.

It can be a good idea for the patient to see individually a different therapist from the one who is working with the whole family. As an anorexic I longed for someone I could confess my deceitful actions to, but I was afraid my parents would hear about it and be upset. Had I been able to confide in a friend or therapist who had no contact with my family, that person might have been able gently to draw attention to the way in which I was deceiving myself, and to help me admit that I did have a problem. It can also be helpful to the family if the therapist involved in family therapy is not the same person the patient has individual contact with. This allows the therapist to take a neutral stance and to help the whole family, rather than to seem to take 'the patient's side'. The family can be seen not only in their relationship to the patient but also as individuals in their own right with their own hurts and anxieties.

A family therapist can help support the parents, who will then be better able to help their child. Parents do need this support, and brothers and sisters often need it too. Watching a young, energetic loved-one starve to death causes unbearable pain. To watch her body becoming frailer and frailer while being unable to save her, or even to understand what is going on, makes the parents feel helpless, inadequate, frustrated, and despairing. They feel guilty, especially as the literature on anorexia appears to point the finger at them (and a few therapists unfortunately do the same). They also feel guilty when they enjoy food themselves while their child will not allow food to stay in her body. The parents are likely to feel that their daughter has rejected not only their food but also them as people. She has become deceitful, and they can no longer trust her. In fact, she no longer seems to be the child they have known. Their loving, happy, 'perfect' daughter has become stubborn and withdrawn, hostile and irritable, especially at meal-times. The parents lose their self-confidence and their trust in themselves and the patient. Depression and anxiety are common, as is anger. Parents may lose all hope for the child's future, and feel that their child is letting them down. Therapy can help the family to turn what looks like an insurmountable obstacle blocking their happiness into a springboard for positive change, allowing them to appreciate each other and to enjoy life together more than ever before.

Parents of girls with eating disorders want to receive information, for example, about the types of treatment and support networks available, advice on what to read, and details about the likely course of the illness. If the child is going into hospital both the patient and the family want support while waiting for admission, combined with details about what will happen in the hospital. A family therapist can provide such support. The therapist can also tell the parents and the patient what to expect during treatment.

Sometimes the mother of an anorexic or a bulimic asks, 'How much should I be making my child eat?' A family therapist will encourage the mother to concentrate on showing the child that she is loved and valued for who she is. This is better than focusing on calories, which can be a way of avoiding other problems and ensuring that the patient becomes increasingly ensnared in her 'food-web'. The more the patient is told to eat, the more reluctant she will be to do so, because refusal is her means of exerting power and control. The therapist may suggest that the relatives help the patient to develop new interests and to think about things other than food and weight.

There can be a lack of trust in the home of a bulimic if the family suspect that she is secretly bingeing and purging. A feeling of suspicion can also develop in the anorexic's household if she does not eat with the rest of the family and is thought to be throwing away or giving to others the packed meals which are prepared for her. The therapist might suggest that the patient should be allowed to prepare her own meals, rather than having to eat what she feels unable to accept at the moment. If she is forced to eat she is likely to become deceitful and develop bulimic tendencies, getting rid of the food after consuming it. The probability of this occurring increases with the age of the sufferer. If the patient is too young to be given the responsibility of preparing her own meals, it may be helpful if her mother and father decide together what it is reasonable to expect her to eat, perhaps coming to an agreement with the patient and a therapist or dietician. The parents should show that they understand how hard it is for their daughter to accept weight gain. After all, she feels both greedy and a failure when she eats, especially if she is not feeling hungry. Although the parents show understanding, they should try to avoid arguments and re-negotiations at the meal table when the patient is given what she has already agreed to eat.

Whatever the treatment approach used (and often a combination of methods is chosen rather than a single approach), it should be recognized that recovery takes time, and so follow-up after the initial course of treatment will be necessary. If you are a patient, you should choose the treatment which feels right for you – if you change your mind you can always switch to an alternative. The important thing is to take that difficult first step, and get some help to defeat the eating disorder before it defeats you.

Useful addresses and books

For receiving help, advice and information:

Eating Disorders Association
Sackville Place, 44–48 Magdalen Street, Norwich, Norfolk, NR3 1JU
Tel: (0603) 621414 for helpline.

EDA has over 3,000 members, who are sent a newsletter every two months. EDA has set up a network of self-help groups throughout Great Britain.

Prevent Laxative Abuse Now (PLAN) Campaign:
Contact the Eating Disorders Association at the above address for details.

British Association for Counselling
1 Regent Place, Rugby, Warks. CV21 2PJ.
(Please enclose s.a.e.)

If you would like to give help, and/or learn how to help:

Anorexia and Bulimia Care, Northern Office
15 Fernhurst Gate, Aughton, Ormskirk, Lancs. L39 5ED.

Anorexia and Bulimia Care, Southern Office
'Arisaig', Back Lane, Monks Eleigh, Suffolk, IP7 7BA.

(The above is a Christian organization, which sufferers and their families may also wish to contact.)

For further reading

Bruch, H., *Eating Disorders: Obesity, Anorexia Nervosa and the Person Within* (Routledge and Kegan Paul, 1974).

Dana, M. and Lawrence, M., *Women's Secret Disorder: A New Understanding of Bulimia* (Grafton Books, 1988).

Lawrence, M., *The Anorexic Experience* (The Women's Press Handbook Series, 1984).

Palmer, R. L., *Anorexia Nervosa: A guide for sufferers and their families* (Penguin Books, 1984).

Partington, D., *Kicking It* (Frameworks, 1991).

Ryan, D. and Ryan, J., *Rooted in God's Love* (IVP, 1992).

Welbourne, J. and Purgold, J., *The Eating Sickness* (The Harvester Press, 1984).

Wilkinson, H., *Puppet on a String* (Hodder and Stoughton, 1984).

Not all these books are still in print. They may, however, be available from your local library (you may need to request them through the inter-library loan system).